ENCORE

BOOKS BY DANIEL FROHMAN

DANIEL FROHMAN PRESENTS
ENCORE

DANIEL FROHMAN

ENCORE

BY DANIEL FROHMAN

LEE FURMAN, Inc. • NEW YORK

To
The People of the Theatre

CONTENTS

[vii]

CONTENTS

CONTENTS

ILLUSTRATIONS

[xi]

ILLUSTRATIONS

ENCORE

ENCORE

One of the greatest pleasures of writing a book is to sit back when it has been published to wait the reaction of the readers. When I finished *Daniel Frohman Presents,* I hoped it would meet with approval. Fortunately, it did. Each reviewer saw the book from a different angle. There was much left out that I should have included, for after all when one has lived for eighty-five years, it is not always possible to find the clothes of one's thoughts as readily as when one is twenty or so. So many sights have passed before my eyes, so many acts, so many scenes. What to write and what not to write are truly weighty problems.

A book grows mellow with the reading even as an old briar pipe grows sweeter with the aging. A house has to be lived in before it takes on an air of comfort. And so it is with a book, the more often it is read, the more interesting it becomes. Broadly speaking every book is a collaboration between the writer and the reader. The reader reads into it his own viewpoints. For each of us a book has a slightly different story. The structure is always the same but the lights and shadows, the tones, the music, the pitch constantly change. And I might take this thought of collaboration a step further. Every man who writes a book of memoirs or opinions virtually collaborates with all the authors who have influenced his life. If he writes of a great personage such as Goldsmith, Kean or Charles Macklin, he is virtually collaborating with all the other authors whose books on the same subjects he has read and whose thoughts and beliefs he has absorbed into his mind. Thus this book is a collaboration. A thousand people have helped me with it. I wish I knew their names so I could write them all down. This, however, is impossible and so I say, to all who have helped me consciously or otherwise, I offer my eternal thanks. The play is almost over but there is still time left for an *Encore*.

FIRST CHESTNUT STREET THEATRE

WILLIAM E. BURTON AS BOTTOM THE WEAVER

1

EARLY DAYS OF THE AMERICAN STAGE

1

THE FIRST organized theatrical company played in New York in 1732 but little is known about it, and perhaps it is as well for it made scarcely a dent in theatrical history. It was certainly not outstanding either for its good plays or its good acting. In 1750 Otway's *The Orphan* was played at a coffee house in King Street, Boston. The leading actors were two Englishmen. The balance of the cast was made up of young men of the town. Though *The Orphan* was one of the first plays ever acted in America, it was at this time almost a century old. Since 1680 it had been a favorite in Great Britain and so I make no excuse for writing a few words about the author.

Thomas Otway was the son of the Rev. Mr. Humphrey Otway, Rector of Wolbeding, in Sussex, and was born at Trotton in that county, March 3rd, 1651. He was educated in Wickeham School, Winchester, and became a commoner of Christ Church, Oxford in 1669. He remained at the University until 1674 when he left and proceeded to London. Soon after he became a player, but I am afraid a rather indifferent one, equipped with no attributes greater than desire and enthusiasm. He appeared in only one play, *The Jealous Bridegroom,* and thereafter retired to the wings to emerge no more as an actor. Otway was a brilliant conversationalist and was able to attract a host of friends. His wit was akin to that of Oscar Wilde who was to be born several centuries later. It charmed everyone. Next, through the influence of his friend, the Earl of Plymouth, he secured a cornet's commission with the troops and served in Flanders. His brilliance as a fighter was scarcely greater than his ability as an actor, so he quitted the army and searched about for something else to do. Tom Otway had never been very provident and not infrequently he was hard-pressed to purchase food or a night's lodging. In desperation he commenced writing, and it was but logical, since he had been an actor, that he should write for the stage. And now at last he was successful. It is said that his comedies are much too licentious but there was no objection to this in the time of Charles II when stage humor was very broad and blunt. In tragedy, however, he excelled and a hundred years or more ago it was said of him that few were his equal in touching the passions. He wrote charmingly of love, but unfortunately not charmingly enough for his plays to endure. They have long since vanished from the boards, unable to stand the competition of Shakespeare whose plays have grown more popular with the years. Otway wrote for his day and age, even though his plays were popular for a century. Shakespeare wrote for eternity. When there were few playwrights, Otway was popular, because of dearth of material. When there were many playwrights, his plays faded. Whereas with Shakespeare, the more plays that were written, the

[2]

greater did he appear by comparison. Of him, Taine has written, "Never was seen a heart so quivering to the touch of beauty, of beauty of every kind, so delighted with the freshness and splendor of things, so eager and so excited in adoration and enjoyment, so violently and entirely carried to the very essence of voluptuousness. . . . Shakespeare flies, we creep. Hence comes a style made up of conceits, bold images shattered in an instant by others still bolder, barely indicated ideas completed by others far removed, no visible connection, but a visible incoherence; at every step we halt, the track failing; and there, far above us, lo, stands the poet, and we find that we have ventured in his footsteps, through a craggy land, full of precipices, which he threads, as if it were a straight-forward road, but on which our greatest efforts barely carry us along. . . . Shakespeare accepts nature and finds it beautiful in its entirety."

Meanwhile what has become of Tom Otway? Has he become lost in Shakespeare's shadow? Shakespeare says to modern actors, "You can make all the success possible in your modern plays, but when you come to me, I will find you out." And he might say the same to dramatists.

But it was not only in comparison to Shakespeare that Otway was not very favorably regarded. Contemporary poets of his day thought little of his ability. He had many failures though he fashioned a dozen plays, made numerous translations and wrote scores of poems. His complete works were published in three volumes in 1757 but unfortunately that was too late to do him any good. For

[3]

Tom Otway died ignominiously in an ancient house, known by the Sign of the Bull, on Tower Hill, April 14th 1685. He was hiding out at the time, afraid to show himself on the streets, in an effort to avoid his creditors. There is a legend to the effect that his death was occasioned by the fact that for days he had not eaten. He was starving and in despair. Then somehow or other he procured a hard, stale loaf of bread. Falling upon it eagerly, the first mouthful caught in his throat and choked him. In his emaciated condition, he could not stand the spasm of coughing that followed, and so he died.

But not all the great men of his day held his writings in disdain for the following advertisement appeared in a newspaper called, "The Observator," November 27th, 1686: "Whereas, Mr. Thomas Otway, some time before his death, made four acts of a play; whoever can give notice in whose hands the copy lies, either to Mr. Thomas Betterton, or to Mr. William Smith, at the Theatre Royal, shall be well-rewarded for his pains."

I have given so much space to Tom Otway because I believe it is his due, since it was his play, *The Orphan,* that appealed so greatly to American colonists. Undoubtedly others of his plays were presented as well. And so, I salute Tom Otway, who a hundred years after his death, helped to give the toddling American stage a new impulse.

2

Competent authorities agree, as for example Watson Nicholson, Oscar Wegelin and Arthur Hornblow, that

[4]

the first known performance on any American stage was given by Anthony Aston sometime between the years 1702 and 1705. Actors before that time, there undoubtedly were but unfortunately they are gone, leaving not a trace. So to Tony Aston the title of First American Actor must go, and on excellent authority, that of Mr. Aston himself. Somehow or other I am rather glad about this for it imbues the American drama with a certain swashbuckling romance. For in the strictest sense of the word, Tony was a stroller, a vagabond, a bon vivant, a loiterer in wine-shops and above all a wandering minstrel under the moons of many countries.

Anthony Aston was the author of: *The Fool's Opera: or the Taste of the Age, written by Mat Medley, and performed by his company in Oxford; to which is prefixed a Sketch of the Author's Life, written by Himself."* It was published in London in 1731.

"My merry hearts," he writes, "you are to know me as a gentleman, lawyer, poet, actor, soldier, sailor, exciseman, publican in England, Scotland, Ireland, New York, East and West Jersey, Maryland (Virginia on both sides of Cheesapeek), North and South Carolina, South Florida, Bahamas, Jamaica and often a coaster by all the same. . . . My father was Richard Aston, Esq., principal of Furnval's Inn, and Secondary of the King's Bench Office—and, tho' a lawyer, lived and dy'd an honest man. My mother was daughter of Col. Cope of Drumully Castle, County of Armagh, Ireland. As for my relations everywhere, I don't care a groat for 'em, which

[5]

is just the price they set on me. . . . I was educated at Tamworth in Staffordshire, and was an unlucky, idle clerk, first to Mr. Randal of the Sixth-Clerk's Office and afterwards to Mr. Paul Jodril. . . . Instead of copying bills I was prone to making verses, reading plays, and instead of going to proper offices I went to see Thomas Dogget, make comical faces in the last two acts."

Anthony Aston was seven years old when he wrote his first poem which fortunately has been preserved. Though it has frequently been quoted before, I am quoting it again for the benefit of those of my readers who have never chanced upon it. It was called: *In Praise of Peace.*

"Once in a fight, when standing at his Ease,
Did boldly eat a piece of Bread and Cheese;
His Fellow asked him for a little Crumb,
Tho' not so big as Supernaculum.
The greedy Dog deny'd: why should he grudge it?
He had above a Peck within his Budget:
But while his Hand cramm'd Meat into his Gullet,
His Mouth received a spightful leaden Bullet.
Now Bread and Cheese lies trampled on the Ground,
And such another Piece can ne'er be found;
So I'm resolv'd I never War will make
But e'er keep Peace for Bread and Cheese's sake."

According to the manuscript of Anthony Aston, he arrived in America in 1701, "after many vicissitudes at Charles-Town, full of lice, shame, poverty, nakedness

[6]

and hunger—turned player and poet, and wrote one play of the subject of the country."

Later he sailed from Charleston on a voyage fraught with adventure. "I embarqued," he writes, "on Board a Sloop of 95 Tun, one Reynolds, Master, for Corotuc, on N. Carolina. Off Cape-fear had the wind at N.W., a frightful Storm; we scudded with Bare Poles a-fore the Wind, when I was lash'd to the Helm to steer for twelve Hours. . . . Well, our Vessel was knock'd all to pieces, as were all the clothes wash'd off me; I was cast a-shore in the River Stone, and was reliev'd by Mr. Allen, who cloth'd me, and honest Abraham Waights fed me for a Month. I went again to Charles-Town, and got a frank passage for New York on board a sloop of Wessel Wessels, Cabus Kirkstead, Master; but being in November, the Nor-wester blew us from the New York coast. As soon as we snuff'd the Land, which after nine Day's Boxing, we were glad to gain the Capes of Virginia, put into Little Mori, hire a Boat acros the Bay into Nauhcoke River,—was courteously entertained by one Hickes, an India Justice of the Peace and a Quaker; he was a convict, and one of Whitney's gang,—married his Mistress (a Widow). He lent me, Dick Ogelthorpe and Lewen (both passengers), Horses to Newcastle in Philadelphia. We lay at Story's—enjoy'd—rode through Elizabeth-Town and so in the Packet to New York."

In New York, he says, he spent his time "acting, writing, courting, fighting—that winter."

What type of play did Tony Aston present in New

[7]

York? This we can only surmise. It was undoubtedly the same sort of thing that he had for some time been presenting in England. He himself called it a *Medley*. It was composed of short humorous scenes from celebrated plays, and between each scene a song or dialogue of his own composing. His English company was composed solely of his wife and son. Each town they visited, he took over as his own. He was very much disturbed if any other company of players were acting the same night. He had no hesitancy at protesting loudly and vigorously. Not infrequently his disturbance had the desired effect. The other and more timid manager delayed his opening a night or two. Despite his arrogance and bravado, however, he was not always successful. Meals were often meager. Sometimes they missed their cue, and failed to make an appearance. In New York, Tony Aston undoubtedly followed his usual repertoire. I do not believe it is known who else played in his New York company. It would be pleasant to record that he took New York by storm but records do not prove it. Undoubtedly he met with indifferent success, otherwise he would have left more than a line about his New York adventure. Broadly speaking, not only was Anthony Aston the first actor to perform in America, but he was the first to present vaudeville in America for that is what his variety presentation really was.

To me, Anthony Aston will always seem a romantic figure, somewhat akin to François Villon and I am surprised that someone does not use him for the hero of a play. He was a good actor, though a much better actor off the stage than on, a swashbuckling stroller, a minstrel who wrote his own songs, laughing, singing, drinking his way through life. He drank life to the full and enjoyed its flavor.

Two of the greatest mysteries about Tony Aston are the dates of his birth and death. That he was born, is conceded. The year was probably 1682. The year of his death is open to dispute. Some writers give it as 1749, others as 1751. Still another claims that he met him on the street in 1753.

And so it is that nobody can definitely say he ever died at all. Perhaps he is still walking the earth, enjoying plays, the music of laughter, anticipating the incredulity that he would cause if he played his greatest part by strutting out onto the stage of Times Square, sweeping off his hat and saying, "I am Anthony Aston." For after all if Shakespeare has lived over three centuries, what is there so odd about another player living scarcely two? Personally, I am very broad-minded. If Tony Aston is still around I want him to know that my studio is always open to him.

3

Joseph Addison's *Cato* was acted in Philadelphia in 1749 according to George Seilhamer whose *History of the American Theatre* from 1749 to 1797 is recognized by everyone as the most authoritative in existence for the particular period it covers. It had been his intention to carry the record onward to the year his work was published, 1888, but death intervened.

When I was cashier and publisher of a daily paper called, "The New York Standard," owned and edited by the famous John Russell Young, there was employed in the Editorial Department a very capable man named George O. Seilhamer. He was a lazy and indolent-looking chap, but very clever with his pen. In those days "The New York Standard" which was published every morning was very much pressed for funds and I had a hard time raising money to carry on its financial activities. Instead of paying Seilhamer his salary of seventy-five dollars per week, I had to give him ten or fifteen dollars on account, just as I did with other members of the staff. One of our editorial writers was sent by Mr. Young as a special correspondent to Cuba and as he had been deprived of his full salary for some time, he felt very joyous over the fact that I was compelled to raise enough money to pay him what he was owed by the paper and also to advance him two weeks' salary so that he could go off on his journalistic mission.

Seilhamer, even though he had to draw his salary in dribs and drabs, was in sympathy with my efforts to keep the paper going. Even Mr. Young himself was unable to draw what he wanted. Seilhamer was always interested in the theatre and although we had a dramatic critic, he occasionally wrote special articles about theatrical oddities which were the prelude to his later published, *History*. The source of his information was the files of

Colonial and Revolutionary newspapers and a tedious task it was for most theatrical notices were brief. Newspapers of those days deemed it degrading to open their columns to the goings on of low comedians and tragedians. There were no dramatic critics. That is why it is so hard to find authentic early theatrical data. All that is known could be crammed into a few volumes while in England the drama was hailed with acclaim. Actors and actresses were admitted to the best society. In the days of Shakespeare, the actors at the Globe were known as the King's company. They were under the patronage of the king. As I have said before, Queen Elizabeth was friendly to the drama. So later were the Stuarts.

But in America, minds were still puritanical. The Colonists were straight-laced. They gave no applause, and yet the situation was droll, too, for many people must have frequented the drama or it wouldn't have survived. Nevertheless, everyone believed that the country was headed for the devil and stopping at numerous way-stations en route. Some of the verbal blasts against the theatre were worthy of political fanfare. It was charged among other faults that it drew vast sums of money from the weak and encouraged idleness. But its chief peril lay in the fact that people were liable to grow fond of it. What greater disgrace could there be than to grow fond of the Drama? It was almost as iniquitous as being a victim of scruples during the World War.

This low opinion in which actors were held in those

early days reminds me of a joke that was told during that same period.

Some strollers being lately taken before a magistrate in the county, one of the company named Kearns was first examined, and being asked his name, replied, "It was Bajazet, last night."

"And what is your profession?" interrogated the justice.

"I play all the tyrants in tragedy."

"And what do you get paid?"

"Seven shillings a week, your honor, and find my own jewels."

In 1750 the General Court of Massachusetts passed an act forbidding plays to be performed. In 1759 Philadelphia followed suit. They added a fine of five hundred pounds to be levied on any manager breaking the law. Rhode Island was pleased with the progress other communities were making and so, by an act of Providence, plays were outlawed in 1761. As a result of all this moral indignation and enforced sanctity, the drama flourished in America until it grew to be a major industry.

The company that acted *Cato* in Philadelphia in 1749 was made up partly of actors from England and partly of local amateurs. It was headed by Thomas Kean and the house at which it played was "Plumstead's General Store." There were few regularly constructed theatres in America at that time, although an excellent one had been erected in Williamsburg, Virginia as early as 1716, another in New York City in 1732 and a third in Dock Street, Charleston, South Carolina in 1736.

But though the store-theatre was unpretentious, the play, *Cato,* was of considerable magnitude. It was first presented at Drury Lane Theatre, London and received the plaudits of Sir Richard Steele and Alexander Pope. In fact Pope wrote a prologue to the play, while the epilogue was written by Dr. Garth. *Cato* was founded on history. "Of a work so much read," says Dr. Johnson, "it is difficult to say anything new." But being Johnson, he had to say something. Therefore he voiced his opinion in eulogy. Another writer declares: "It cannot, however, surely be thought an ill compliment to the author, to confess, that although as a play it may have many superiors, yet it must ever be allowed to stand foremost in the list of our dramatic poems."

Even though *Cato* has long since vanished from the stage, of one thing there can be no doubt. It was an auspicious play for Thomas Kean to undertake at "Plumstead's General Store."

Thomas Kean appeared for the first time in New York on March 5th 1750. He was the leading player of the Murray and Kean company. How good a player he was is open to conjecture. But there is no denying his ambition. By profession, Kean was a writer. He therefore had a choice—either he could starve as an actor or as a writer. But another member of the company, John Tremaine, a professional cabinet-maker, undoubtedly saved the day many times by selling a specimen of his

[13]

handiwork when they were unable to procure a theatre. It is well for all strugging actors and authors to have a small business on the side to fall back on. What could be more lyrical than a delicatessen shop?

Thomas Kean was the first actor to present *Richard III* in America. With a bow to Seilhamer, I quote the following hand-bill which was given out by members of the company on the afternoon of March 5th 1750. This was the first time that Shakespeare was presented in America.

ADVERTISEMENT FOR MARCH 5, 1750
By His Excellency's Permission
At the Theatre in Nassau Street
This evening will be presented
The Historical Tragedy of King Richard III
Wrote originally by Shakespeare and altered
by Colley Cibber, Esq.
Pitt, 5s. Gallery 3s.
To begin precisely at Half an Hour after
6 o'clock, and no person to be admitted behind the
scenes.

Thomas Kean presented plays valiantly throughout the entire season, but financially his endeavors were not very successful, despite the fact that his performances were usually crowded and he had no hesitancy to sell more tickets than there were seats. Frequently patrons arrived to find they were unable to secure entrance to the small theatre. Perhaps it was due to the general

[14]

resentment that was flaming up about him, that he announced before the end of the season his retirement permanently from the stage on the advice of several gentlemen of the town who were his friends. In the future he intended to devote himself exclusively to writing.

2

EDWIN FORREST

1

EDWIN FORREST was born March 9th 1806 in a small house in the Southwark section of Philadelphia. His father was a Scotchman, a native of Dumfrieshire, a man of good birth and heritage but having few of those material possessions upon which cardboard people set so great a store. By trade he had been an importer of Scotch fabrics, but several years previously he had failed in business, whereupon he had accepted a position in the old United States Bank. Later when this bank closed, he had gone to work for the Girard National. In 1795 he had married Rebecca Lauman who, though of German descent, had been born in Philadelphia. Of this union, seven children were born. The first died in infancy. The six that followed were named Lauman, Henrietta, William, Caroline, Edwin and Eleanora.

The Forrests were very poor, living humbly and practicing the sternest economy. William Forrest was oppressed by the debts which his failure had left dangling over his head. Still he plodded on, believing that ultimately all would be well. Both he and Rebecca were very religious. It worried them that they were only able to give their children a meager education. But to Edwin this neglect was of small importance. Genius can educate

[16]

EDWIN FORREST

MACREADY AS HENRY IV

itself. He was thirsting for knowledge. Curious about everything. He had an expressive voice, vigorous, force-ful, entirely free from affectation. Often he used to go home from the Episcopal Church of which they were members, and mimic Dr. Joseph Pilmore whose impos-ing manner greatly impressed him. His memory was marvelous. He was a born actor.

One of the first persons to recognize that Edwin Forrest had a spark of genius in him, was an old family friend, the famous ornithologist Alexander Wilson, whose pictures of birds and descriptions of nature fas-cinated the small boy. Wilson, on his part, was no less fascinated by the way Edwin recited the *Shepherd Boy of the Grampian Hills.* It was Alexander Wilson who taught Forrest several of the better poems of Robert Burns and did much to lead the boy's mind into paths of good literature. This new interest was a splendid spur to the boy, and each time he learned a new piece, he could scarcely wait to repeat it to his devoted friend.

William Forrest died in 1819 at the age of sixty-two, leaving little behind him in the way of worldly pos-sessions but a good name. Rebecca Forrest, though stunned at the tragedy that had befallen her, was a woman of firm character, steadfast, brave, courageous. Not permitting grief to conquer her, she opened a small millinery shop, assisted by her two elder daughters. Meanwhile the boys went to work. Edwin's first job, which he kept only a short time, was in the printing office of the "Aurora." Later he worked in a cooper shop,

[17]

then for Mr. Tiers, a ship-chandler on the wharf. Finally he secured a position with Baker and Son, Importers. He was very ambitious, brilliant beyond his years. In his spare time he studied Shakespeare. His employer was very pious, with a long, gloomy face that never cracked a smile. Because he was a pillar of the church, he imagined he had to wear a stony look. In mournful tones he used to warn Edwin of the pitfalls of the stage. Alas, that there was no one to warn poor Mr. Baker of the pitfalls of bigotry.

Several years before this, when Edwin was about ten years old, accompanied by his brother William, he had joined a Thespian Club. He and his fellows took their enterprise very seriously and often acted in barns and woodsheds. The price of admission was five pins, an apple, a handful of raisins, or what have you. The proprietors were quite willing to enter into negotiations over the matter of admission. And their possessions must have taken on an air of affluence for the shows were well-attended. It is to be doubted if the whole state of Pennsylvania could show a group of boys with a finer collection of marbles. "But," you ask, "could they act?" They used to ask the same thing about Mrs. Siddons and John Philip Kemble. The annals of the stage leave no doubt of their ability, nor can there be any doubt of Edwin Forrest's greatness. He was the most typical of all American actors. Few have ever approached him. I daresay, however, that in 1816, during his Woodshed Theatre exploits, his acting may have been somewhat spotty and

[18]

did not nearly approach the finish that he later attained when he was at the peak of his career. But then, too, for a ten-year-old tragedian he left little to be desired.

Edwin liked nothing better than to visit the old South Street Theatre, long since torn down, with its huge pit surrounded by a double row of boxes. It was here that Edwin made his first public appearance on any stage at the age of eleven. It came about quite by accident in this manner. While Edwin was playing marbles with some other boys in front of the theatre, Charles Porter, the manager, happened to come along. He paused and watched the game. Edwin aroused his interest and so he asked him if he could perform the part of a girl in a play. Edwin gulped, "Yes, sir." His answer would have been the same had he been asked to play the part of an ostrich, a hippopotamus or Mahomet's mountain. Mr. Porter explained that the girl who was supposed to act the part was sick. The play was to open the following night and there was no chance of her being well enough to appear. Thereupon, Mr. Porter gave Edwin a play-book to rehearse the part. I can imagine with what elation Edwin sped home to make known the joyful news. For him, it was the thrill that comes once in a lifetime. It did not take him long to learn the part but the procuring of a costume was somewhat of a problem. In this, to some extent, his sisters helped out. One of them gave him an old turban for a hat. Another supplied him with a bit of cloth for a bodice. He decided to use bits of scenery for a skirt. That night he was too excited to

[19]

sleep. Over and over again he repeated the words of his part. Then the next night came, overcast, ominous. He was to take the part of Rosalia di Borgia in the romantic melodrama entitled, *Rudolph* or *The Robbers of Calabria*. Before going out on the stage he gazed in a mirror and decided that he needed more curves and so he hastily slipped a few bits of tapestry into his bodice. But unfortunately he hadn't caught a glimpse of his feet. His skirt was too short. His shoes were anything but those of a girl. He presented a very ludicrous appearance.

A boy in the gallery cried out, "The heels and the big shoes! Hi yi! Hi yi!"

Edwin scowled. Forgetting himself, he completely stepped out of his character. Gone was Rosalia and in her place was a small boy choking with anger. "You wait till this play is done, and I'll lick the stuffins out of you!" he cried.

The audience was convulsed with laughter, the curtain was brought down and Edwin was hustled ignominiously from the stage.

But his debut was not entirely a failure at that, for he kept his word, met the boy, who had annoyed him, in the alley afterward and bestowed on him a sound thrashing, and my, how those stuffins flew!

2

Though his first stage appearance was a dismal failure, Edwin refused to be beaten. And so he tried again. At the age of thirteen he acted Young Norval at the

Tivoli Garden but with indifferent success. Then a year later, at the old Walnut Street Theatre he played the same part in a splendid stock company, supported by old Warren and William B. Wood. The date was November 27th, 1820 and it is an important one for it marks the real start of Edwin Forrest as an actor to be reckoned with. His efforts were well-received but still he was not satisfied.

And so on December 6th of that same year, we find him writing a letter to Mr. James H. Caldwell at New Orleans. "Sir: Having understood you intend to open your theatre in the city of New Orleans some time during this month, I, by the advice of a number of friends, have taken the liberty of addressing you relative to an engagement. I am desirous of performing in your company for six or eight nights, in such parts as I shall name at the foot of this letter. . . . I acted last season in Messers. Warren and Wood's Theatre for a few nights, and drew respectable and profitable houses, which is a difficult matter to do at this season in Philadelphia. For my capacity I refer you to the managers above named, or to Colonel John Swift, of this city. Should you think it troublesome to write these gentlemen on the subject, I will procure the necessary papers and forward them to you. If you conclude to receive me, I should like to hear on what terms, and so forth. Address me care of John R. Baker and Son, 61 Race St., Philadelphia, Yours truly, Edwin Forrest. Characters: Douglas, Octavian, Chamont, Zanza, Zaphna, Tancred."

The letter was fruitless. He never received an answer.

In September 1822, the proprietors of three theatres at Pittsburgh, Lexington and Cincinnati came to Philadelphia for the purpose of engaging a company of players. Forrest applied to Jones, the manager, and must have made a good impression for he was given a position at eight dollars per week. A reckless spirit of adventure was always strong within him and he eagerly looked forward to his first trip west.

On October 10th, 1822, he wrote his mother a letter from Pittsburgh: "Dear Mother: I arrived here yesterday about eleven o'clock and am much pleased with the place and its inhabitants. I was quite out of patience riding so long in the stage over such tremendous mountains, but was greatly delighted, on reaching the summit of them, to view the surrounding country,—so vast and varied a landscape. . . . Pittsburgh is three hundred miles from Philadelphia. It is a sort of London in miniature, very black and smoky. The Alleghany River and Mountains surround it. The theatre is very old. . . . This, you know, is the first time I have ever been away from you. I have felt many qualms of homesickness, and I miss you, dear, dear mother, more than words can give out. Has William gone to Petersburg? Furnish me with every particular, especially how our Tid is, and whether she reads with the yard-stick. Give me an account, too, of my Grandma and of my *beautiful* Sister. The long ride in the stage has made my hurdies so callous that they would ward off a canon-ball. . . . Give my respects to all my friends, particularly to Philip. Inform me also if you can, how the Tivoli Garden gets on. Write as early as possible, and pay the postage as I am out of funds. I expect the managers by the next stage. Mr. Hughes, formerly of the Walnut Street Theatre is here. I find him a perfect gentleman. Your affectionate son, Edwin Forrest."

The Pittsburgh engagement was short but successful. Soon the company packed up its properties and luggage and engaged passage for Maysville, Kentucky, on one of the Ohio River flat boats. The trip was leisurely, made at a snail's pace. Now they were in a country where time had ceased to be important. If a thing couldn't be done today, what matter? There was always tomorrow. Nevertheless, it was living! The air was fragrant and the nights were bitingly cold. The trip took five days of drifting through lovely scenery. Time was passed in singing, playing games, dancing and telling jokes.

At Maysville they played a few evenings. The returns were very satisfactory. Thence on to Lexington where they started a long engagement in an excellent theatre. There were few empty seats and the audience was extraordinarily intelligent.

The season at Lexington closed on February 22nd, 1823, after which the company started across country for Cincinnati. It was a long and hazardous journey. The women made the trip in covered wagons; the men rode horseback. They opened at the old Columbia Theatre, Cincinnati March 6th 1823 in *The Soldier's*

Daughter. The next night they offered *Richard III.* Moses Dawson, editor of a Cincinnati newspaper, wrote: "Edwin Forrest has a finely-formed and expressive countenance, expressing all the passions and marvelous exactness and power, and he looks the character of Richard much better than could be expected from a person of his years. He assumes a stately majesty of demeanor, passes suddenly to wheedling hypocrisy, and then returns to the haughty strut of towering ambition, with a facility which sufficiently evidences that he has not only deeply studied but also well understood the immortal bard. The scene with Lady Anne appeared to us unique, and superior to everything we have ever seen not excepting Kemble or Cooke. In the soliloquies he uttered the sentiments as if they had arisen in his mind and we never once caught his eye wandering towards the audience. Of the tent scene we do not hesitate to say that it was a very superior piece of acting. Horror and despair were never more forcibly represented. We consider Mr. Forrest's natural talents of the highest grade, and we hope his good sense will prevent him from being so intoxicated with success as to neglect study and industry. We are willing to render to youthful talent a full meed of praise; but while we applaud, we would caution. Applause should not be received as a reward, but as an incentive to still further exertion to deserve it."

From Cincinnati the company went on to Hamilton, Lebanon and Dayton but with indifferent success. They had received their laurels. Now their popularity was on the wane. At Dayton, being unable to meet expenses, the company disbanded. Shortly afterward they re-formed but to little purpose. Their subsequent history is of little importance as far as Edwin Forrest is concerned. He was anxious for better things. Then suddenly James H. Caldwell offered him a job in New Orleans at eighteen dollars per week. Eagerly accepting it, he imagined that Mr. Caldwell had at last remembered the letter he had written him in 1820. This was not the case. Caldwell had been impressed by Forrest's acting in Lexington. He had been in Kentucky for a brief visit. At once, he had decided to make Edwin an offer.

Edwin's first appearance in New Orleans was at the American Theatre in the rôle of Jaffier in *Venice Preserved,* February 4th 1824, Caldwell sustaining the part of Pierre. New Orleans at that time had about thirty-thousand inhabitants and was the social capital of the South.

It might be interesting to note here that the first English company that ever visited New Orleans performed in a room in St. Philip Street, in the year 1817. In 1819, Mr. Caldwell paid the city his first visit with his company and occupied the St. Philip Street Theatre, later known as the Ball-room. In 1822 he came again and occupied the Orleans Theatre, playing alternate nights with the French company. French plays, naturally, were acted prior to the English.

The Camp Theatre, or rather Amory Hall was erected in the year 1823, by the enterprise of Mr. Caldwell.

Therefore he must be considered the Father of the Drama in New Orleans. And in 1824, as has already been set down, his company was joined by Edwin Forrest, thereby making theatrical history. For Forrest was welcomed gladly by everyone in this gayest of American cities. It was here that his real fame began. So extreme was his success, Caldwell grew somewhat jealous and commenced casting him in old men's roles. Edwin however made no objection. He worked diligently to master these new parts. It was all part of his education. For that same reason he lived for awhile with the Indians in order that he might depict the Indian on the stage more exactly. But no matter how hard he tried, he was unable to satisfy Caldwell. Finally they quarrelled bitterly over a girl. Forrest challenged his employer to a duel but Caldwell treated the matter lightly and refused to accept. However, it was the end of his New Orleans days. But now it was no longer hard for him to secure engagements. He had made a reputation for himself. And so in 1825, he returned North to accept an engagement in Albany, under the management of Charles Gilfert, an eccentric Dutchman, who ran a stock company. It was his custom to have various visiting stars play the leads. Edwin agreed to play any subordinate rôle that was given him. In this fashion he was thrown in contact with Edmund Kean whom he greatly admired. Forrest played Iago to Kean's Othello. Kean was very enthusiastic, and extravagant with his praise.

"Henceforth," he declared, "Iago must always be played in this manner."

3

And now a word about the old Bowery Theatre in New York City. In 1825 Barriere saw one of his greatest dreams begin to materialize, the building of a theatre at the head of the Bowery under his direction. The site was then known as Bull's Head and was owned by Henry Astor. Barriere died before completing his enterprise and the building was finally erected in 1826 by a company of wealthy persons, consisting of Henry Astor, Samuel Gouveneur, James Hamilton and Thomas L. Smith. They were desirous of securing the best talent obtainable. They had heard of Edwin Forrest and the triumphs he was leaving behind him everywhere. He was then acting in Albany under the management of Charles Gilfert. By a peculiar coincidence they had decided to offer Mr. Gilfert the managership of the Bowery Theatre. Prosper M. Wetmore who was connected with the new theatre project was delegated to go to Albany to make the necessary arrangements. He watched Forrest act and was deeply impressed. It was not hard to secure Mr. Gilfert's services for he had failed completely and was unable even to pay his actors. Edwin, always a heavy spender, was destitute. In despair he was forced to pawn his costumes in order to secure enough money to get to New York to fulfill his new engagement at the Bowery, which was not quite finished. I imagine

[27]

Mr. Wetmore would willingly have advanced Edwin the necessary money but undoubtedly Edwin did not wish his new employer to know the true state of his finances. He wanted to pose as a man of affluence, though it was a hard part to act on an empty stomach.

Edwin sailed down the Hudson, hardly able to wait for his new engagement to begin. Arrived in the city he took a room in a tavern on Cortlandt Street. He was very miserable. He had neither friends nor money. Not for a moment did he dream of writing to his mother for help. Added to this, he was desperately homesick. Then suddenly everything changed. One day on the street he met an actor named Woodhull who was arranging a benefit for himself at the Park Theatre. Edwin, always the most generous of persons, offered his services free. "I'll play the part of Othello," he said. When the evening of the benefit came, the house was only half full but the audience was friendly. In the middle of the pit sat old Gilfert, toying with his snuff-box. The performance could not have been more enthusiastically cheered, whereupon Gilfert hastened behind the scenes to congratulate Edwin. It was then that the hungry Forrest broke down and confessed his poverty. Gilfert promised to give him sufficient money next day to pay all his debts. He kept his word and with the money thus received Edwin returned to Albany to redeem his wardrobe. Afterwards he played one night in Washington, and six nights at the Star Theatre, Baltimore. From his earnings he was able to send his mother four hundred dollars.

The Bowery opened the last week in October. On the following Monday, Forrest made his first appearance in Othello. The house was crowded with an eager audience, still vividly remembering his triumphs at the Woodhull benefit. At the close of the performance, Edwin was personally congratulated by the stockholders of the new theatre. They met in the Green Room and tore up his contract which called for twenty-eight dollars per week. In its place they gave him a new one for forty dollars. After that crowds flocked to the Bowery to see him and his name became a household word. A few months later, when his contract with Gilfert had expired, Forrest played elsewhere and his salary was two hundred dollars per night. It was a pretty good salary for his day and age. He had just passed his twenty-first birthday. Now wherever he went, he was a success. Success dogged his footsteps and went before, like a thick velvet carpet upon which he walked with the step of a conqueror.

Meanwhile Mr. Gilfert was very successful managing the Bowery Theatre until in 1828 it was entirely destroyed by fire and Gilfert died of a broken heart, due to his losses. During that same year the house was rebuilt and Thomas S. Hamblin assumed the management. He continued prosperously to direct its affairs until 1836 when it was again destroyed by fire, believed to have been the act of an incendiary. Dinneford rebuilt it but he failed to make it successful. In 1839 it burned again and again was rebuilt. Hamblin resumed management and during the first season produced the spectacular

Last Days of Pompeii by Bulwer-Lytton. In 1846 it burned again and was rebuilt in exactly eighty-four days. This time A. W. Jackson was the lessee and manager. He made a fortune and retired to enjoy his wealth. Hamblin again took the theatre over. On his death, I. P. Waldron, formerly treasurer, became lessee but he wasn't very successful and had to take Captain Smiley in as a partner. On Monday evening, June 30th 1856, the Bowery Theatre opened under the management of Mr. John Brougham, a rollicking, fun-loving, mirth-provoking Irishman, full of wit and good humor, a clever author and actor, a successful dramatist and a good manager. He was a man of excellent education having been graduated from Trinity College, Dublin. The old Bowery had been completely altered, refitted, painted and decorated and beautified generally. It presented an appearance of lightness and elegance. The plays performed were *The Married Rake* and *Macbeth*.

I have gone thus into detail about the Bowery Theatre because it is undoubtedly one of the most important houses in American theatrical history. I imagine there must be a volume devoted entirely to its fascinating history. If there is, however, unfortunately I have not run across it.

4

On February 5th 1827, Forrest commenced an engagement at the old Federal Theatre, Boston, and it was during this engagement that he met James Oakes. Thereupon a friendship began which was to last for forty years, a friendship the like of which it would be hard to duplicate. Oakes was twenty at the time of their meeting and at once elected himself to be a sort of press-agent for Forrest, without portfolio and without salary. In the following years Forrest turned often to him for guidance and was never disappointed.

On February 7th 1827, Forrest wrote the following letter to his mother: "Sunday evening I arrived, after a tedious and wearisome journey, at the place that is called the literary emporium of the Western hemisphere, and on Monday evening, for the first time in my life, made my bow to the good people of Massachusetts. I was received with acclamations of delight, and the curtain fell amidst repeated and enthusiastic testimonials of gratification and approval. . . . Here, mother, I must break off awhile; for Mr. Fisher, a Quaker preacher, has just stepped in to see me. He was one of my fellow-passengers hither in the stage-coach; and as he is a very agreeable man, possessing much mind, I have a disposition to treat him with deference and respect."

He continued his letter later: "Evening, eleven o'clock. I have just returned from performing William Tell. The house was crowded and the applause generous. I am charmed with the Boston people. They are both liberal and refined. In this place I shall add much to my reputation, as well as enlarge my purse, and at present, this latter is as necessary and will be as acceptable as the former. . . . Why does not brother William write me oftener than he does? Did you receive the hun-

[31]

dred dollars I sent you? . . . All court, every attention, is paid me here by the young men of first respectability. These flattering attentions make me hold you, beloved mother, dearer than ever before. I trust I shall not live in vain, but hold my course a little longer, that I may restore you to peace and competency and reflect a mellow light upon the evening of your declining days. . . . With sincerest love for sisters and brothers, I am yours till death, Edwin Forrest."

5

The first engagement of Edwin Forrest at the Park Theatre, New York, began on September 15th 1827. He opened as Damon, later appearing as Hamlet, Lear, Iago, Macbeth, Brutus and Carwin. Of *The Tragedy of Brutus,* the dramatic critic of the old "New York Mirror" wrote as follows: "Of Forrest's personification of Brutus we cannot use language that would be thought too laudatory by those who witnessed the effort; though we are sure that the dictates of our feeling and of our judgment would not meet the approbation of those who have not—as it is scarcely credible to what a height of excellence this young tragedian has arrived." And the rest of the New York City papers played the same refrain with scarcely a varying key.

Another critic, describing him, wrote: "Edwin Forrest has handsome, regular features. He is the greatest actor America has ever produced. He is about five feet ten inches tall, splendid of figure, though perhaps a trifle

JOHN BROUGHAM AS SIR LUCIUS O'TRIGGER

MRS. D. P. BOWERS AS QUEEN ELIZABETH

too heavy and powerful. This makes him seem out of place in parts such as Hamlet but he is very graceful nonetheless. He seems to breathe forth abundant health, but this good health is due entirely to his own unceasing efforts. Up till the age of nine, Forrest was a thin, pale child. He had a slight forward stoop to his chest and shoulders. Although courageous and impulsive, he had a quick pulse, was nervous and very sensitive. Tears came easily to his eyes. His father was often worried about him. Then a circus came to town. As usual Edwin and his pals were breathless with excitement. They tried to walk the tight-rope, to turn somersaults, to do tricks on parallel bars and to wrestle. Long after the circus had departed the boys were still attempting their stunts, nor did Edwin cease until he had perfected them. By the age of seventeen he was in rugged health, a fit specimen to go with a medicine show. Of course he never did this, but in after years he frequently bragged that he had once worked in a circus and had later been a minstrel. . . . Edwin Forrest has a marvelous voice. He is superb in elocution. He works long hours to perfect his parts to the minutest details. His inflection and enunciation are beyond compare. If there is a better King Lear anywhere else in the world, let him come forward."

6

Forrest made his first professional appearance in London at the Drury Lane Theatre on the evening of October 17th 1836 in the rôle of Sparticus. The house was crowded for he was famous in England long before his arrival. Of that performance, "The Courier," the next morning, said, "America has at length vindicated her capability of producing a native dramatist of the highest order, whose claims should be unequivocally acknowledged by the mother country; and has rendered back some portion of the dramatic debt so long due to us in return for the Cookes, the Keans, the Macreadys, the Knowles and the Kembles, whom she has, through a long series of years, seduced, at various times to her shores,—the so-long-doubted problem being happily solved by Mr. Edwin Forrest, the American tragedian, who made his first appearance last night on these boards, with a success as triumphant as could have been desired by his most enthusiastic admirers on the other side of the Atlantic."

7

Edwin Forrest married Catherine Sinclair in London on June 23rd 1837. Catherine was nineteen years old, the daughter of John Sinclair, a well-known vocalist. On their return to the United States, a dinner was given him at the Merchants Hotel, North Front Street, Philadelphia at which two hundred were present. The happy couple had then been married six months.

8

It was during Forrest's second tour of Great Britain that the famous controversy with William Charles Macready began. Macready had made a successful tour of America in 1843. Macready never held the position of actor in great esteem. He was more or less ashamed of his calling, even though he was an actor of great brilliance. He was never popular with the multitudes but by the more cultured members of society he was well received. He made a great deal of money but occasionally his press notices were a bit sour. At this time he and Forrest were very good friends and during his two or three weeks engagement in New York he stayed at Forrest's New York home. Mrs. Forrest was very fond of Macready. She still remained friendly toward him when his feud with her husband had grown very bitter.

Edwin made his second appearance at Covent Garden, London, a few months after Macready's return. On February 17th 1845, as Forrest appeared in the character of Othello, he was greeted by hisses which broke out simultaneously in three different parts of the house. The disturbance seemed to have been well-organized. It successfully drowned out every sincere attempt of applause. The next evening Forrest played Macbeth to even greater opposition. The press notices during this engagement had suddenly ceased to be as uniformly friendly as they had been on his first visit to England. "Mr. Forrest's Othello is a burlesque," one paper said, and several others made similar comments. A few nights later, of the production of Macbeth, John Forster wrote, "Our old friend, Mr. Forrest, afforded great amusement to the public by his performance of Macbeth on Friday evening at the Princesses. Indeed, our best comic actors do not often excite so great a quantity of mirth. The change from an inaudible murmur to a thunder of sound was enormous, but the grand feature was the combat in which he stood scraping his sword against that of Macduff. We were at a loss to know what this gesture meant till an enlightened critic in the gallery shouted out, 'That's right, sharpen it!' "

Many other journals, however, refused to be influenced by personal chagrin, and warmly praised his acting. Speaking of Macbeth, The Athenaeum said, "Mr. Forrest's former manner has received considerable modification and become mellowed with experience." The Sun called his Lear, a decisive triumph, "Those contrasts in which he delights, all tell well in the character of Lear, and they were used with excellent discrimination and great effect."

It was Forrest's firm belief that all hostility could be directly traced to Macready. This may not have been true but certain it is that Macready was an intimate friend of Bulwer-Lytton who refused Forrest's request to appear in his two plays, *"Richelieu"* and *"The Lady of Lyons."* Forrest was unable to get an audience with Mitchel, in Paris. Mitchel was the manager of the English Theatrical Company. To Edwin this was very humiliating because he had told his friends in America he would appear in Paris before returning. Many Parisians were clamoring to see him. Meanwhile the flames of anger were fanned by the undrafted soldiers in either camp.

[36]

After leaving London, Edwin toured the United King-
dom and was received everywhere with acclaim. His
reception in Glasgow and Edinburgh was notable. It
was like welcoming home the son of a favorite son for
Edwin's father had come from Dumfrieshire. One night
while Macready was playing Hamlet in Edinburgh,
Forrest stood up in a box and deliberately hissed him
and that powerful hiss echoed everywhere throughout
the house.

Forrest returned to America, hating Macready. But
Mrs. Forrest did not share her husband's disdain. She
was still very fond of him.

9

Rebecca Lauman Forrest died June 24th 1847 at the
age of seventy-three and Edwin was broken hearted. To
his friend, James Lawson, he wrote: "My mother is dead.
That little sentence speaks all I can say, and more—
much more."

10

Macready came to New York in 1849 under the management of Mr. Niblo and James H. Hackett. A warm
reception was planned for him by some of Forrest's
friends who arranged with the famous gangsters, the
Bowery Boys, to have him driven from the stage. Edwin
heard of the plan and vetoed it at once. He would have
no part in it. Nevertheless, he hated Macready and
missed no opportunity to insult him. Of a celebrated

actress whom he did not like, Edwin used to say, "Her face looks as though Macready had sat down on it."

On May 7th 1849, the Astor Place Opera House was crowded with hoodlums. Macready was overwhelmed with hisses. On the evening of May 10th Forrest was acting *The Gladiator* in the Broadway Theatre when Macready was attempting *Macbeth* in Astor Place. This night the house was jammed by friends of Macready and the Bowery Boys were far outnumbered. A great mob had collected in the front and rear of the theatre which the police were unable to handle. Finally the 7th Regiment and the National Guard were called out. The crowds refused to take the reenforcements seriously. The soldiers were greeted by hoots and catcalls. The riot increased. The mob was armed. Bricks were tossed at the soldiers. A few guns barked out. Several soldiers were wounded. Mobs are always without minds. General Hall gave the order, "Fire!" One musket shot rang out. The crowd roared with laughter. The derision increased. It was a critical moment. General Sanford said, "Fire!" Only three shots followed. They did absolutely no good. Then Colonel Duryea shouted, "Guards, fire!" The answer was a volley of musketry. When the smoke had cleared away there were thirty dead and many severely wounded.

Neither Forrest nor Macready was very proud of the way their private feud had ended, and in justice to both of them, I believe it should be said that neither was to blame for the way their quarrel ended. Neither of them could have foreseen that what started as a private grudge would end in virtual civil war.

Toward the end of their lives the two great actors were no longer enemies.

That year 1849 was a bad one for Forrest in many ways, for in April, Catherine, his wife, left him and took up a separate abode. On February 16th 1852 commenced the famous Forrest divorce case which shocked the country because of the violent way both plaintiff and defendant tossed charges at each other. The testimony fills a volume of twelve hundred pages but no discussion of the case can be made here. Our concern is solely with that of Edwin Forrest as an actor, his youth, his struggles and accomplishments.

Forrest had many friends and at the same time perhaps more enemies than any other American actor. His hatred was a terrible thing; his love, devotion and tenderness, almost divine. In the days of David Garrick, they used to say, "He who has never seen Garrick has never seen a drama performed." The same might likewise be said of Edwin Forrest.

3

TEMPERAMENT

TO SUCCEED on the stage, one must have temperament. There is a distinction between this and intelligence. To illustrate: The great Rachel in her youth had to have the subtleties of some of her leading roles explained to her by her stage manager. But when they were made apparent, she illustrated every nook and cranny of the part she was impersonating with her tremendous luminous dramatic nature. Temperament is like electricity; perhaps it is the same. We can tell what it is like, what its manifestations are; yet we cannot clearly define it. Perhaps it is nearer akin to the subtle quality called genius than is intelligence. It seems to be the faculty of knowing things without learning them.

Crudely speaking, it is the power to grasp, to sympathize, to respond, the quality that enables one to incarnate the outline or sketch of the author's fancy, to reach out into ether, as it were, and draw therefrom a definite human being of flesh and blood, of emotions and passions. It manifests itself in what is called personal magnetism, a charm that makes the audience feel. An ignorant woman may possess it in a marked degree, while to a well-bred, highly educated girl it may be wholly foreign. In every social set or village may be found at least one man or woman distinctly gifted with magnetism. It may be the quality of being lovable. At any rate, it will be found frequently that such a one is a leader.

While temperament and art are a good team, certainly the former is the more indispensable. Clara Morris ruled the New York stage for years, less through her art than by reason of her splendid emotional gifts, which in moments of supreme passion compelled her audiences to vibrate with either sympathy or with terror.

Salvini, by far the greatest foreign artist who ever visited this country, made art a religion. Though capable of enthralling an audience by the force of his personality alone, he never would undertake to play a part without having studied it for years. He refused to play King Lear until he had worked and pondered on the rôle in all its phases for a decade. It is said of this tragedian that he used to go to his dressing room at five o'clock in the afternoon and begin making ready for the part he was to play in the evening. He required that every detail be arranged to promote realism, even candles being provided since their light was more natural and sunlike and did not produce the pallid effect of gas. Bit by bit, as he put on his make-up, he hypnotized himself into the character he was to impersonate. So complete was his incarnation of Othello, so passionately did he reflect the racking emotions of hatred and jealousy, that his own nervous system was taxed even as was that of the Moor himself. This is why he played the rôle only at intervals. How Shakespeare would have enjoyed the great Italian in this part! He would probably have said, "Surely this is not my Othello, but something greater than I ever dreamed of!" Thus it may be claimed that dramatic art in its highest form is creative, rather than imitative.

The first performance of a part may be an adequate achievement; but it is seldom perfect. With developing temperament, the actor builds up the rôle nightly until it becomes an incarnation of the author's ideal. Misdirected temperament is about as dangerous to its possessors and those roundabout as is a locomotive without a driver.

When Macready was playing in New York many years ago, a cowboy, possessed of the notion that he could act, so persistently begged the tragedian for a chance to show what he could do that at last he was given an opening. He was to take the part of the king, a minor rôle in the play, and he worked it for all it was worth. His strut was kingly, his scowl sovereign. This was good in a way; but he carried it too far. The stage director had indicated the spots where each of the combatants in the duel were to fall, the one in the center of the stage being reserved for the star. But the novice coveted the limelight, and, being king, decided to possess it. So, being mortally wounded, he fell in the center of the stage.

"Move over!" growled Macready *sotto voce*, giving him a sly kick.

But the cowboy never budged. "Confound you!" muttered the tragedian in a voice low, yet hoarse with menace, "move over! You're on my spot, I tell you!"

TEMPERAMENT

The sharp kick that accompanied the words roused the cowboy, and he raised himself on his elbow and roared back, "Look here, Macready, I'm king in this here drammer, and I'll die where I darn please!"

That was temperament with a vengeance; yet the man lacked the prime essential—intelligence.

It was said of the elder Booth that under certain conditions the illusions of the drama became so real to him that it was unsafe to engage in a stage duel with him.

Probably nothing is more common in a manager's experience than the recital by female aspirants of their many stage qualifications. They have been well-educated, have made a study of the drama, have been taught to recite, and all the rest of it. Yet a vast majority of them are lacking in the essential quality—temperament. True, personal presence, grace of action, voice and culture contribute largely to a woman's success; but if she has not the vital fire somewhere in her make-up, latent perhaps, but capable of development, she need not hope to succeed on the stage.

And many seem to feel that acting means simply the speaking of lines, the fitting in with the machinery of the plot. This is only the apprenticeship of the stage. It is the function of dramatic art to bring out the highest quality of player and play. Spoken lines are only one of the means of expression. Salvini could do as much with his eyes as with his lips, standing for what seemed endless periods, his tongue mute, while he looked the whole gamut of emotions,—hatred, contempt, humor. This art

[43]

means the portrayal of human nature with photographic accuracy. Clara Morris was apt to do something new every night, so continuously did her rôle develop as she played it. If, during a tirade of passion, she chanced to see a pin on the carpet, she would stoop to pick it up with a touch of feminine realism that was marvelously convincing. Edwin Forrest's every gesture expressed a thought. Once he complained of the manner in which a supernumerary placed a chair at a table.

"Do it this way," said the star, suiting the action to the word.

"Do it that way!" retorted the man keenly appreciating the subtle touch of the master. "I wouldn't be working here for a beastly three dollars a week if I could do it that way."

"If that's all you get," said Forrest with a show of disgust, "do it any blooming way you please!"

Dramatic temperament is essential to all kinds of performers, vaudeville, musical comedy, burlesque, drama, grand opera and Shakespearean. Weber and Fields, Montgomery and Stone, Sam Bernard, Anna Held, Lillian Russell, Fay Templeton and other musical comedy magnets rose from the vaudeville stage, while the burlesque-drama developed such artists as Mansfield, Nat Goodwin, Harry Dixey and Francis Wilson.

In England and France also many of the great exponents of the drama at one time or another in their lives lent their talents to a lighter form of entertainment. In fact, it is a rule of the drama—with only exceptions enough to prove it—that important actors and actresses have begun in a modest way. And why not? **The nearer** the bottom one begins, the more firmly grounded, deeply rooted he will be. Nature doesn't allow seeds to flower away up in the air; why then should actors be expected to do so?

BROADWAY

BROADWAY IS a street of memories. When I was a boy of fourteen working in the office of the New York Tribune, Barnum's Museum was at the corner of Ann Street and Broadway. Later it burned down. Thereafter Barnum built a new museum at Broadway near Canal Street.

Barnum was very wily and shrewd. He was a man of fine character, honest, straightforward, dependable.

At this time the principal theatres were below 13th Street. The Broadway Theatre was on Broadway near Broome Street where traveling stars used to play their engagements. I have never forgotten the fine acting of Mrs. D. P. Bowers in a play called *Lady Audley's Secret*. Mrs. Bowers had a long and successful career both as an actress and manager. She was a prime favorite in Philadelphia, celebrated for her Shakespearean rôles and was on various occasions in the companies of both Edwin Booth and Salvini.

The Olympic Theatre was on Broadway near Houston Street. Here I saw George L. Fox, famous clown from the Bowery, play a burlesque of Hamlet. He was an uproariously funny comedian. One night Edwin Booth went to see him. Hamlet was one of Booth's greatest parts and no doubt he was anxious to see if he could get any new pointers.

Harrigan and Hart's Variety Theatre was at 444 Broadway about the time that Tony Pastor had his famous playhouse on the Bowery. Some years later Tony Pastor moved up to East 14th Street between the Academy of Music, which was then the chic resort of grand opera, and Tammany Hall. At Tony Pastor's, May Irwin and her sister, Flo, made their early appearances. So did Lillian Russell. Tony Pastor was a man of fine character. He was noted for his dress-coat, his opera hat and his unruly forelock. The variety shows offered by Tony were the funniest in town. He was one of the original board of "The Actors' Fund of America."

Harrigan and Hart afterwards moved to 18th Street at Broadway. Edward Harrigan was a fine old actor who popularized Irish, Negro and German plays, using the tenement house districts as a locale. He wrote most of his own plays and acted in them with his partner, Tony Hart. Harrigan's son and daughter are now well-known actors on Broadway. The daughter married Walter Connolly who has achieved success both on the stage and in pictures. Every part he essays is a finished portrayal. His naturalness is amazing.

When Tony Hart died, Harrigan continued on alone as a star but in the course of a few years he, also, passed away.

For many years the principal theatre in town was Wallack's at 13th Street and Broadway, controlled by the famous actor-manager, Lester Wallack, who was considered the handsomest actor of his day. His theatre

[47]

featured well-known English comedies. I used to pay my thirty cents Saturday nights and watch them from the galleries. Later Wallack moved uptown to 30th Street and Broadway. During this period, 14th Street and Broadway was the center of the town.

One of the most famous theatres in America was Niblo's Gardens on Broadway near Prince Street. It was originally called the Sans Souci but earned its greatest renown as Niblo's. A hundred years ago William Niblo used to bring his customers from the Astor House by special coach, which was, I think, an innovation worthy of any age. Here played some of the greatest actors in the world, Edwin Forrest, Charles Kean, William E. Burton and Charlotte Cushman. Charlotte Cushman was an amazing woman for she had few of the physical requisites to be an actress. She had neither beauty of face nor figure, yet somehow when she acted, the audience fell under the spell of her charm and personality. She played with a sincerity that came right from the heart, and so she appeared beautiful, an inner beauty that all recognized.

It was at Niblo's Gardens that *The Black Crook* was performed in 1866. It created a sensation. It aroused not only the consternation of the moralists but the resentment of the clergy who inveighed strongly against the performances because so many of the ballet girls danced in short dresses and displayed their legs from the knees down. The preachers everywhere spoke against the immodest display, and proved such good press-agents that

TOMMASO SALVINI AS OTHELLO

CLARA MORRIS AS MISS MULTON

the show ran for four hundred and seventy-five performances. *The Black Crook* was nevertheless a brilliant spectacle and brought in a new era of gay performances.
There was a leading singer in it who impressed Richard Grant White, father of Stanford White, the architect.
After witnessing her performance, he declared that she
had a voice of "vocal velvet." This alliterative phrase
spread like wildfire throughout the country and made
the singer famous.

Afterwards the Karalfy Brothers presented their great
spectacle, *Around the World in Eighty Days* at Niblo's.
Subsequently many well-known plays were presented at
this house including a few of my own productions.

Harry Hill's famous night club, the first of its kind,
was located on Houston Street near Broadway. Here
there were singing, dancing and plenty of drinking.

Wood's Museum was way uptown near 30th Street.
It was here that Lydia Thompson's Burlesque Troupe
appeared. They had come from London. Miss Thompson
was a handsome woman and her presentations created a
sensation. In the course of time, Augustin Daly took over
the Museum and renamed it The Augustin Daly Theatre, and so it remained until his death in 1899 when I
took over the house while they were building the new
Lyceum. Under his management appeared such famous
artists as John Drew, Otis Skinner, Maxine Elliott, May
Irwin, Clara Morris, Fanny Davenport and Agnes Ethel.

The Weber and Fields' Music Hall was next to
Daly's. At Weber and Fields' appeared Sam Bernard,

[49]

De Wolfe Hopper, William Collier and Lillian Russell, besides of course, Joe Weber and Lew Fields. It was a resort of uproarious comedy and was always crowded. Delmonico's Restaurant was then at 14th Street and Fifth Avenue. It afterwards moved to 26th Street and Broadway. Opera was given at the Academy of Music at Irving Place. Here as a lad, I used to sell librettos and give the profits to the chief usher. This enabled me to hear the operas for nothing. Next door was Steinway Hall, the Carnegie Hall of that period, where the great musical artists appeared. It was here that I heard the great Rubenstein at one of his recitals. Across the way was Lent's All Year Round Circus. On Irving Place was Irving Hall where musical artists also appeared. Later it became the German Theatre under the management of Herman Conreid. Conreid rode the waves of success until eventually he directed the destiny of the Metropolitan Opera House.

At West 23rd Street and Sixth Avenue was Edwin Booth's gorgeous and commodious playhouse. Still further west, at Eighth Avenue was the Grand Opera House, controlled by those picturesque financiers, Jim Fiske and Jay Gould. French opera was for a long time popular at this place and toward the end of each season the Broadway attractions came over to play a week's engagement at this house, at popular prices, exactly as though it had been out of town. Augustin Daly and A. M. Palmer sent their companies over there for a week's engagement annually. I did likewise.

At Madison Avenue and 28th Street was the Garden Theatre, where Lillian Russell at one time appeared in opera and where *Trilby* was first given with Wilton Lackaye and Virginia Harned. My brother Charles and David Belasco also had considerable success here with Blanche Bates in *Under Two Flags*. And it was here that Col. Henry W. Savage presented *The College Widow* for an entire year.

On Broadway at 28th Street was the old Fifth Avenue Theatre where Augustin Daly produced many of his plays. One of them which had a long run was *Pique* with Fanny Davenport as the star. It came at a time when he needed a success for he was then also running the Grand Opera House. A few years later Daly moved to his own theatre then as now known as Daly's and I became the manager of the Fifth Avenue Theatre when the famous J. H. Haverly leased it.

A popular little playhouse called the Bijou was opposite Wallack's Theatre. It was here that Henry E. Dixey played *Adonis* for six hundred nights. It was a sensational and delightful show. In his support was Amelia Summerville who was known as *The Merry Little Mountain Maid*.

Then came the Casino, established by the late Rudolph Aronson, where comic opera was the rage, where Francis Wilson starred for a year in *Erminie* and where Lillian Russell, Jefferson d'Anglais and other celebrities appeared.

In September 1871, Sheridan Shook and Albert M.

Palmer established their famous Union Square Theatre on East 14th Street. It was here that the famous Vokes family first appeared in America, in their variety acts. Thus Shook and Palmer contributed much toward the establishment of vaudeville in America. But the house did not devote itself for long to variety. The management turned to more serious plays and in doing so made theatrical history. Both Shook and Palmer believed that any play worth producing was worth producing well. They were of the opinion that good scenery and good casting were as important as plot. It was an excellent partnership. Shook was the proprietor, Palmer was the manager.

At the Union Square Theatre some of the greatest stars in our profession used to appear. They produced many world famous plays. One of them was the best-constructed play ever presented on any stage. It was called, *The Two Orphans*. Palmer's leading man was Charles R. Thorne. The leading lady was Rose Eytinge. Thorne was one of the greatest actors of his time. He played with dramatic force and without the usual ranting which was common among many stars at that time. The reason that ranting was so common in those days was because the gallery was the most important part of the theatre. Unless the actors made a great noise on the stage, the people in the galleries held back their approval. They believed that an actor should speak loudly. Now that we have no galleries the method of the actors is more reserved. Thorne was the first actor of his time to know that great effects could be reached without too much physical and emotional upheaval.

The leading lady, Rose Eytinge, who afterwards became a star in Shakespearean rôles, was a splendid actress. She was a black-eyed, black-haired Jewess. One day when she came to rehearsal Thorne said to her, "Miss Eytinge, the way you look at me, one would think that you were going to eat me." She replied, "Have no fear, Mr. Thorne, my religion forbids me from doing that." I mentioned this story once to Clara Morris, greatest emotional actress of her time. She said, "Some years ago when I was starred in *Camille* I had a leading man who was very sensitive and temperamental. He was a good actor but he thought that nobody in the company liked him. That was not true. We had no reason to dislike him. It so happened that I had a great liking for celery while he detested the sight of it. One night in New York when I came on as Camille and he was playing Armand Duval and making love to me, through some error on the part of my maid, I was not wearing a camellia on my breast, so I went to the supper table and picked up a piece of celery. I held it toward him and made the flower speech. When he saw the celery he thought it was a deliberate insult. Turning, he left the stage in anger and the curtain had to be rung down. Unfortunately it was the same night that the comedian set fire to the ice cream."

John Stetson was well known throughout the profession. He had the Globe Theatre in Boston. He was very deliberate but a capable business man. His Boston partner was Isaac B. Rich who also owned "The Christian Science Monitor," while Stetson owned "The Police Gazette." In 1880 I was the manager of the old Fifth Avenue Theatre in the employ of J. H. Haverly. Haverly was a brilliant producer. He liked to speculate, to plunge heavily. He had companies and theatres throughout the country but he was always in need of money. He had numerous other investments including large holdings in Colorado mines. When he controlled the Fifth Avenue Theatre, he wanted to borrow sixteen thousand dollars and so he sent me to Boston to see John Stetson. In the meantime Stetson was trying to get the Fifth Avenue Theatre away from Haverly, but it was a profitable house and Haverly would not let it go. Nevertheless he sent me to Boston to borrow the money from Stetson in order that he might transmit it to Colorado to protect his holdings there. I saw Stetson at ten o'clock in the morning. He gave me the check and I immediately telegraphed the money to Mr. Haverly. When I called back on Mr. Stetson some time later, to say good-bye and thank him again, he roared with resentment and anger that he wanted to stop the check.

"Why should I lend Haverly sixteen thousand dollars when he won't give me the Fifth Avenue Theatre?" he asked.

But I told him that the check had already been cashed and the money sent to New York.

Haverly had a shrewd way of sizing up the characters

of his competitors. He sent me to Stetson who was rough and tough because I was quiet and mild-mannered. In like manner he sent his rougher and tougher managers to borrow from the milder business men. He was excellent at appraising the ability of the men working under him.

Henry Irving played at the old Star Theatre at 13th Street and Broadway, formerly Wallack's, during the blizzard of 1888. No snow-storm in the city's history ever attained such prominence as that one. New Yorkers are proud of it. Press agents have been boosting it ever since. They toss stories of it about as though they are making open challenges to Alaska and Greenland. Even though I remember it well, I still don't believe that any snow-storm ever could live up to the reputation of that blizzard. At that time, it seemed to me that its greatest defect was that it prevented people from getting to the theatre. At my old Lyceum we could not give a performance because the snowdrifts were so great our actors couldn't get through them. The old theatrical truism, "The show must go on," was crowded out by the elements who changed the wording to "The snow must go on." And it did with considerable enthusiasm. But Henry Irving was not in as bad a predicament as we were for his company lived at a hotel close to the theatre. At the time he was playing to enormous business. He knew that if he gave no performance the box-office would have to refund a great deal of money, or else exchange the tickets for some other night. So great was the business, that was practically impossible. Under these conditions, therefore, he gave the performance to an empty house, thus relieving himself from any obligation to the people who could not get there that night.

Through the years I have met a great many people on Broadway. I remember the time when Henry E. Abbey announced the first appearance of the famous Lily Langtry in America at his Park Theatre. Just before she was scheduled to appear the Park Theatre burned down, and Abbey did not know what to do. It seemed as though her appearance would have to be deferred indefinitely. There had been a large sale of tickets and to avoid disappointing the public, Lester Wallack generously placed his theatre at her manager's disposal. It was a gesture quite in keeping with Lester Wallack's character. Abbey accepted the offer and Mrs. Langtry made a great success.

Henry Abbey, like myself, came from Ohio. He was a bold, enterprising manager who with his partner, managed many stars and traveling companies. He also became the manager of the Metropolitan Opera House, a position he continued to hold until his death.

A. M. Palmer afterwards left the Union Square Theatre and became the manager of Richard Mansfield. He lost his money in various speculations and died a poor man. His wife, Mrs. A. M. Palmer was at one time a famous actress. After Palmer died I got up a benefit for her and turned over four or five thousand dollars to her. In appreciation of this service she gave me an onyx scarf

)in which her husband used to wear and which I still
use.

Augustin Daly, whom I regard as the greatest of all
American managers, used to be a dramatic critic and
had his articles about the theatre appearing in six different papers, weekly and evening, but he had a strong
leaning toward the theatre. He wrote a play called *The
Flash of Lightning* which he produced in the old York
Theatre at Broadway and 8th Street. It was a great success and he continued in management. From his company there came such famous actors as Fanny Davenport,
Clara Morris, Ada Rehan, John Drew, Otis Skinner,
Agnes Ethel and others. Daly produced many amusing
German comedies and then he went into Shakespeare
with Ada Rehan and John Drew. When he died in 1900,
I took Daly's Theatre and moved my old Lyceum Company there. He had a great theatrical library and when
his books were put up at auction, I bought a great many
of them for my collection at the Lyceum. Daly had a
habit of keeping track of everything that happened to
the members of his company in a personal and business
way. He rehearsed his own company. He was the first
man at the theatre in the morning and the last man to
leave at night. When Clara Morris was the leading lady
of his company she was getting thirty-five dollars a week.
She asked him one day whether she couldn't receive
more salary. He refused, and she intended to leave the
company, or so papers announced. Daly came to the
theatre early one morning and, looking through the mail,

he saw a letter addressed to Clara Morris from Wallack's
Theatre Company. He surmised that Wallack was going
to engage her so he took the letter out and told the door
keeper that when Miss Morris came in to send her up to
him, and then put the letter back when she had left the
stage door. When she arrived, he agreed to give her the
salary she asked, fifteen or twenty dollars more a week.
She signed an agreement with him and then went down
and got her mail. When she opened the letter from
Wallack's, she found it offered her twice as much as Daly
was paying her. So he kept her until she became a star
in her own right, as many others of his company did.

John Drew left Augustin Daly's company and went
under the management of my brother Charles when he
began to spread himself in theatrical work. He made
John Drew a featured player and he engaged Maude
Adams, who was then in my company, as Mr. Drew's
leading lady. Ethel Barrymore made her first appearance
on the stage in a small part in a play with John Drew and
Maude Adams at my brother's theatre. The play was
called *Rosemary*.

There is an actress living in London whose name is
May Fortesque. When I first took the old Lyceum in
1886, she was having a law suit in London and got a
judgment in her favor of fifty-thousand dollars in a
breach of promise case. The result was printed in papers
all over the world. I wanted to fill in six weeks' time
at the Lyceum before I began my productions, so I com-

municated with her and offered her an engagement for
that period of time. She sent me word that she would
not appear for less than twenty weeks, so I took her for
six weeks at the Lyceum and fourteen weeks on tour,
as I did not wish to begin my career with the average
traveling attraction. I wanted something unique, distinguished, and she belonged to the aristocratic class of
artists whom I wished to present at the old Lyceum.

After that I began my productions with my first play,
The Great Pink Pearl. But I will say nothing more about
my activities as I have spoken about my enterprises in
my recent autobiography, *Daniel Frohman Presents*. My
brother, Charles Frohman, like myself, began his career
as an advance agent. He represented a small dramatic
company which played throughout the country. After the
Haverly Minstrels, he managed the Wallack-Dillon
combination. Then he started companies of his own and
produced the famous play *Shenandoah*. After that he
took the Empire Theatre and organized The Empire
Theatre Company. He not only had a company but he
had a number of stars. He was far more enterprising
and active than myself. Many of the actors and actresses
who appeared at the Empire Theatre had appeared
with me, such as Henry Miller, William Faversham,
May Robson, Henrietta Crosman, Maude Adams and
others. The first play he produced was by David Belasco
and Franklin Fyles. Fyles was dramatic editor of "The
New York Sun." Charles sent the manuscript to me to

[59]

read and asked if I could give him a title for the play. I liked it and named it *The Girl I Left Behind Me.* The leading man in that play was William Morris, the father of Chester Morris, who is now in pictures, and the leading lady was Sidney Armstrong, who was followed by Viola Allen.

Now the theatres began to move uptown as the town enlarged until they reached far up Broadway and into the side streets such as 46th and 48th and so on. Since my early days I have seen many changes in the geography of the city, especially on Broadway. I remember the horse cars and the time when women wore such voluminous skirts that a favorite amusement used to be to watch them try to squeeze themselves into the cars. In those days the telegraph was the new invention and the inventor, S. F. B. Morse, had sent the first telegram, from Washington to New York, four famous words, "What hath God wrought." Now we have subways, motor cars, telephones, radio, and heaven knows how much further the world will go in other inventions for the benefit of mankind, but nevertheless, human nature is always the same. Costumes and customs may change but man and his aspirations, his ambitions, and his hopes for happiness remain the same. We have always been human beings with human emotions. The reason *The School for Scandal* is always a success is because Sheridan, the author, treated the follies and foibles of mankind not only as they existed in his time but before his time and

s they exist in the present. The object of life is to gain
happiness, but the means of obtaining happiness differ
widely and it is the conflicts that help to make interest-
ng dramas.

5

OLIVER GOLDSMITH

1

OLIVER GOLDSMITH's life was as interesting as any of the works he wrote, for he was a man of many diverse moods and temperaments, the victim of an unshakable belief in his own inferiority. He attempted to play a tragedy part in a comedy vein and so there was discord. In all the annals of English literature he is one of the most lonesome of men.

In appearance, he was insignificantly ugly. An ugly giant inspires awe but there are only smirks for pygmies. He was under medium height and looked like a servant hovering about for a tip. Low forehead, face round as the moon and like the moon pitted with spots and crevices. But unlike the moon he did not shine by reflected light, not even when he basked in the warmth of the mighty sun—Samuel Johnson.

Goldsmith was slovenly, uncouth. He was guilty of many absurdities and impudences. But his impudence was a mask that he wore to cover his timidity. What we admire in Goldsmith above all things is his humanness. He continually bickered with his publishers. His appetites and passions were violent. Not infrequently he secured advances from booksellers for books he had planned. Then he dallied over their completion. But

vithal he was always willing to help a friend who was in
trouble and everyone who was in trouble was his friend.

He was one of the greatest men of his time, greater
far than any of those who turned away from him into
oblivion. Those who offered him friendship are still
remembered.

2

Oliver Goldsmith was born November 10th 1728
in the village of Pallas, County Longford, Ireland. His
father was a minister with a mind that was dressed in
velvet even though his body was arrayed in clothes that
were threadbare. The family consisted of five sons and
three daughters. Oliver was the second son, seven years
the junior of Henry.

It was to Henry that Oliver's first great poem, *The
Traveller,* was dedicated. Thus does he pay tribute to his
brother:

"Where'er I roam, whatever realms to see,
    My heart untravell'd fondly turns to thee:
    Still to my Brother turns, with ceaseless pain,
    And drags at each remove a lengthening chain."

It was not odd that Goldsmith should have become an
author for his family believed in education. His first
teacher was Mistress Elizabeth Delap who for more than
half a century taught the children of the neighborhood
the intricacies of letters and arithmetic. It was her fond
boast till the day of her death in 1787 at the age of
ninety that she had placed the famous Doctor Goldsmith

[63]

on the highroad to knowledge. He was only three year
old at the time and pretty much of a rascal. Though she
bragged about him in after-years, at the time he greatly
vexed her and often she doubted whether she would be
able to do anything with him at all. He was dull and
listless, always falling asleep. But in his sleep he must
have had wonderful dreams for he commenced scribbling
verse before he was able to write legibly. No matter what
else may be said in his disfavor there was nothing wrong
with his imagination.

This imagination was spurred on by Thomas Byrne
into whose hands he passed when he was six years old
Paddy Byrne, as he was called, was the village school
master. He had been a soldier abroad during the reign
of Queen Anne and had risen to the rank of a Quarter
master in Spain. He was, according to Goldsmith, stern
and severe, always ready to tell a joke which the pupils
considered themselves called upon to appreciate. When
he smiled, the sun shone for his scholars. When he
frowned it was cloudy and dismal. But he was con
scientious and no schoolmaster ever tried harder to make
something of the poor material that had been allotted
to him. He was somewhat of a writer, a great mathema
tician, a good enough orator to be a preacher, and in an
argument he usually won because he never knew when
he was beaten. Though vanquished he went on talking
until his opponent fled the field, a victim of sheer ex
haustion.

But as far as Oliver Goldsmith was concerned, Paddy's

From a painting by Sir Joshua Reynolds

OLIVER GOLDSMITH

DR. JOHNSON

greatest merit lay in the droll stories he told about his vagabondage He had wandered in many strange countries and had countless stories to tell of his adventures in the wars. Perhaps like most story-tellers he polished up his narratives, dressed them with interesting scenery, and usually made himself the central figure about whom all the plots revolved. Often, so enthusiastic did he become, he neglected the regular lessons completely and the entire class would go with him down a golden road of imagery, a road peopled by lusty, swashbuckling heroes and gay romance. And though all the others returned to the classroom when the tale was finished, Goldsmith lingered along the way. Even after the class had been dismissed he was still under the spell of a dream. So the seed of wandering, which Goldsmith had always possessed, was nourished and nurtured, changing, perhaps, the whole current of his life.

Among other things, Paddy Byrne taught Oliver all the folklore of the countryside. Every single rock and tree had its legend. Superstition rode about dressed in fine raiment and was a guest to everyone. Fairies, goblins, banshees all were very real. Paddy told legends of the Little People and the boy listened and was charmed. Gradually a certain bond sprang up between the two. They were in sympathy with one another, despite the great disparity in their ages. Paddy, like Oliver, dabbled in poetry. Frequently they tried to fashion little songs together. Oliver wrote countless verses, though scarcely a line of them has been preserved. It was his custom to cast them into the fire after they were finished.

Quite by accident, a few of the papers were discovered by his mother before he had a chance to destroy them. She read them eagerly. They made her very happy for she imagined that some day her boy would be a genius, but how great a genius, I doubt if she ever dreamed in her wildest flights of fancy. It is largely through her efforts that Oliver was given a good education. Perhaps had she not determined on this he might have become an artisan. And it is barely possible he might have had a far happier life had he done so. Education seldom brings happiness. It merely imparts to a man sufficient light to see the vast scope of his limitations.

In 1752 Goldsmith left Ireland and went to Edgeworthstown to attend a college preparatory school under the superintendence of the Reverend Patrick Hughes. He was so full of good spirits that he did not notice the lodging house at which his bags had been left. Not only did he forget the house but he forgot the street as well. Fortunately while he was wandering dazedly around he once more encountered the porter who had helped him with his luggage. And so he found it once more.

This is a typical Goldsmith story and there are many more equally absurd, for he was a poor manager. He was born to be a vagabond, always irresolute, yet friendly and compassionate. His age could not understand him

but through the ages he has grown to be understood.
Perhaps it is true, as Pope has so ironically written, that
"Authors, like coins, grow dear as they grow old;
It is the rust we value, not the gold."

3

On June 11th 1745, when he was sixteen years of age,
Goldsmith entered Trinity College, Dublin. He entered
as a "poor scholar" with a room on the top floor. To
make up for his lack of tuition fee he was forced to do
odd jobs around the college. He swept the courts in the
morning and waited on table. He did not eat until his
fellow students had dined. He even wore a regulation
costume that denoted his poverty. This was a regular
and unexplainable college custom. The costume consisted of a black gown without sleeves and a black cloth
cap that had no tassel. He had committed the immense
crime of being poor and hence this dismal prison-like
garb. Goldsmith, who was of a shy and gentle nature,
hated college under these conditions. To him they were
revolting. It is not to be wondered at, therefore, that he
was only a fair student except in the classics in which he
excelled. To add to his meager fortunes he used to write
street ballads which he sold for five shillings each.

Goldsmith's unhappy university days terminated
eventually on an occasion when he had been chastised
and, as he imagined, publicly disgraced. He was bordering on despair so he left the school, sold his books and
decided to embark on a voyage to America. But his

brother Henry succeeded in bringing about a reconciliation between Oliver and the faculty with the result that he returned to the University to finish his course. Even though he did so, his record was without distinction. Nor had he decided what his aim in life was to be.

Next it was agreed that Oliver was to study law. His uncle, the Reverend Thomas Contarine, loaned him £50 in order that he might proceed to London for this purpose. But on the way, he was inveigled into a game of cards and he lost all he possessed. Utterly penniless he was forced to return home.

Some time later, his uncle supplied the necessary funds for him to go to Edinburgh to study medicine. This was in 1752. But he did not set out seriously on his new studies. Most of his time was given over to conviviality. He remained in Edinburgh for eighteen months after which he set out for Bordeaux.

From the year 1753 onward commenced a period of Goldsmith's life that is amazing, a period of vagabondage without apparent reason or design.

During his first year on the Continent he went to Leyden in Holland where he continued his medical studies at the University. He attended the lectures of Gaubius on chemistry and Albinus on anatomy. But he was unenthusiastic. He was more interested in literature. Besides he longed to be footloose. Inevitably he broke away from school and during the second year he wandered afoot all over Holland, Belgium, France, Switzerland and the northern part of Italy. His sole resources

were one spare shirt, a flute and a guinea. It was not long
before he was reduced to begging his way from door to
door. According to legend he was but an indifferent
player on the flute. Nevertheless with his music he
managed to pick up an occasional coin. He seldom knew
from whence his next meal was coming, or where his
weary head would rest at night.

Sometimes he was welcomed in as a guest of a wayside
cottage. Occasionally he stopped at a priory. And I daresay there were times when he spent the night in prison,
because he had nowhere else to sleep. Many a fight with
postillions did he have when he slept in barns without
first asking permission. But in spite of everything, he was
free. He could tramp the world playing his flute. There
were no ties to hold him back. And wherever he went,
he borrowed money, that is whenever he could talk anyone into loaning him a small amount. This happened
very often, surprising though it may seem.

Goldsmith lived solely for the day itself and gave no
thought for the morrow. His one redeeming feature was
that he could endure privations like a stoic. It was his
custom as he walked through Flanders and into France
to play his merriest tune on his flute. And usually the
music produced him a night's lodging and a flagon of
ale.

4

"There is hardly a country in Europe in which I am
not a debtor," Goldsmith once wrote. It was his policy to
borrow as much and to pay back as little as possible.

He had no sense of responsibility where money matters were concerned, and no debt in his eyes was a debt of honor which he felt he must repay. Rightfully this is usually charged against him when one sets out to make an accounting of his character.

On the credit side of the ledger, however, must be set down the fact that he was the freest of persons. When he had money he loaned it lavishly. He was a friend worth having when one was in trouble but certainly not when one was in funds. Thus it must be said that his affairs were in good condition. He was solvent for there was more gold in his character than dross, and more genius than sense.

Goldsmith was a born vagabond. He dallied with most of the pleasant sins of life and found most of them to his liking. Even though he was born to the cloth, he soon wore it threadbare and he was forced to make himself a new suit. His detractors would have us believe that he made a suit of fool's clothing but those who have studied his character know that the suit he made for himself was of excellent material. It might have appeared to be of common cloth but in reality it was uncommon for it has lasted through two centuries and even today it is not shabby. He was mentally one of the best-clothed of writers.

And yet, with the exception of his brother Henry, his family were ashamed of him. They washed their hands of him. He was hopeless. They had grown weary of his vagabondage, of his profligate ways of living, of the speed with which he squandered his money at cards. He was a failure. They wanted to forget him. And now almost two hundred years later, they are themselves remembered simply because they were related to him.

5

Finally in the course of his travels, Goldsmith arrived in Paris and in some way or other gained admittance into the best society of France. Among others, he met Voltaire. Later he thus paid tribute to him: "As a companion no man ever exceeded him when he chose to lead the conversation. . . . His meager visage seemed insensibly to gather beauty; every muscle in it had beauty and his eyes beamed with unusual brightness."

In this company was Diderot and also Fontanelle then almost a hundred years old. While in Paris he attended the chemical lectures of Rouelle. He also was a frequent visitor at the theatres, especially the performances of the famous Mademoiselle Clairon.

Goldsmith continued his wanderings into Germany and Switzerland. It was from here that he sent his brother Henry, in Ireland, the first rough draft of the poem which was afterward elaborated into *The Traveller*.

He remained in Padua for some time due to the death of his Uncle Contarine who had occasionally sent him money, though never any great amount. The cessation of it was a serious blow to him and in desperation he wrote a pleading letter to Hodson, his brother-in-law. No beggar ever begged alms more abjectly. Nevertheless to this letter there was no reply. Certain historians state that while he was in Padua he took his medical degree. This is open to argument. However, the matter is of no great importance because in those days, although it was nice for a doctor to have a degree, a degree was not essential. The curing of the sick was attempted in a rather careless manner.

Goldsmith grew despondent at receiving no response to his letter. He gave up wandering and once more returned to England, paying his way across France with the notes of his magic flute. They accomplished their purpose even though they were often off key.

6

It was the year 1756 when Goldsmith returned to England, downcast, discouraged, homesick. He felt very badly over his Uncle Contarine's death. The fact that his family ignored him emphasized his loneliness. Suddenly life had become a dreary place and the garret in which his soul lived was bleak and desolate with many dark and sombre corners.

Goldsmith never knew the value of money but he knew the value of home and friends. And although he was inordinately fond of cards, he never knew their value either, else he might have won more often. No matter how frequently he lost, he always returned to play again. Perhaps it is true that if one gets burned often enough, one grows fond of the fire.

When Goldsmith reached England he was penniless

and his flute had lost its voice. No longer did it have the power to secure him a meal as it had in France. Either the English people didn't appreciate good music or they appreciated it too well. The sad truth is that Goldsmith was never more than an indifferent musician.

He attempted to get a job in a country drug shop but his studies at Leyden and Padua availed him naught. Then he turned to the stage and took part in comedies at a country town in Kent. As a result of this experience he wrote *Adventures of a Strolling Player*. It is too bad that a complete record of his stage experiences has not been preserved for us. All that exists are occasional references to them in his writings.

Finally he drifted to London, a rather woebegone figure. His mood even reflected in his writings: "The clock has just struck two; what a gloom hangs all around! no sound is heard but of the chiming clock, or the distant watch-dog. How few appear in those streets, which but some few hours ago were crowded!"

Soon after this he became an usher in a boarding-school, a position which he detested. The head-master was a chronic grouch, the school-mistress disliked him because of his ugly face, and the boys were always playing jokes on him and holding him up to ridicule. It was therefore a pleasant escape for him when soon after he became an assistant in a Fleet Street chemical laboratory. While in London he heard that Dr. Sleigh who had been his classmate in Edinburgh was in town.

After diligent search he located him. Dr. Sleigh

proved to be a real friend for at his instigation and with his help, Goldsmith began to practice medicine in Bankside, Southwark. His patients were usually poor people who were unable to afford a good doctor. Because Dr. Goldsmith was tender-hearted, it mattered little to him whether they had money or not. He gave of his best but it is open to argument whether that best was very good. He longed to move among the rich but he knew he could not until he had made somewhat of a reputation. Goldsmith was always a braggard. He liked to assume a fine cloak of grandeur even though there was no such costume in his wardrobe.

He envied the success of lesser men. He was always inordinately jealous nor did he make any effort to hide his chagrin. On the contrary he paraded it like a banner for everyone to see. No one can study the life of Goldsmith without being sorry for him. He was lonely, hungry, but the hunger was not hunger for food. Even though often he had starved, his hunger of the spirit was far greater than his hunger of the body.

Oliver Goldsmith's knowledge of medicine may have left much to be desired in completeness but he was a clever doctor none the less for he understood men's frailties. Many an imagined disease can be conquered by appealing to man's vanity. Half the illnesses of life, he knew, exist only in distorted imaginations. A *bon mot* or a sonnet ofttimes has more curative value than pills and nostrums. Some philosopher has written that man has perfected so many medicines he is forced to invent diseases to use them up. Which reminds me of a certain merchant who when he was sick, sent for the undertaker. Upon being questioned as to his reason for this, he explained that he did not want a doctor because in all business transactions he hated to deal through a middleman.

In those good old days in which Goldsmith lived, the want of medical qualifications was no drawback to the practice of it. Then as now, most people got well not because of the doctor but in spite of him. A droll story is told of how on one occasion Goldsmith in his guise of doctor went to call upon a patient who was a printer. As a result Goldsmith's position was much improved. He became a proof-reader and for awhile at least his elbows went back into his sleeves again. In his excitement at meeting the printer, Goldsmith forgot to prescribe for his illness and so he got well without any complications setting in.

As a doctor, Goldsmith knew the anatomy of words, the physiology of character. He understood the aches of ridicule and the pains of despair. He could dissect life into multiple glowing phrases. He prescribed the panacea of perfect prose for a world that was suffering from myopia and growing pains. He gave to the *clio medica* of his age one of the greatest poems of all time, a novel that must always rank with the world's best and a comedy never equalled during his age except by Sheridan—surely tonic enough for a world with few newspapers and books, a world of scant education. And in return he was made a butt for all jokes, shunned by almost everyone, a clown with a master's degree, the pen of an angel, and a heart overflowing with woe.

On September 21st 1758 Goldsmith took an examination at the College of Surgeons, London, for the position of hospital mate. He failed in this examination, perhaps because he was nervous, though it seems more likely that his failure was due to lack of knowledge.

Through Dr. Sleigh, Goldsmith secured introductions to various booksellers who employed him frequently at miserable pay. Necessity forced him to be a hack writer but even necessity could not make him write like a hack. Even in his least important writings there are occasional flashes of wit and genius. Through one of the printers with whom he came in contact, Goldsmith met Samuel Richardson, an author of renown who had written such books as *Pamela* and *Clarissa*. Richardson was quite wealthy for he was a publisher as well as a novelist. He became interested in Goldsmith and employed him as a sort of associate editor and proof-reader. Goldsmith attended to these duties while he was waiting for people to get injured or to become sick for he still starved as a physician but swaggered about as though he had an elegant practice. At least he was a doctor of elegant phrases. Some contend that his patients were always sicker than the patients of any other doctor. This may only be legend but it must be said in his favor that all his clients that passed away, passed away in well-phrased deaths.

Through Richardson, Goldsmith met many prominent personages in the literary world including Edward Young, author of *Night Thoughts.* Such associations spurred him on to greater literary effort.

7

One of the greatest errors Goldsmith made in all his life was to incur the wrath of David Garrick who was then undisputed Emperor of the Drama. Garrick's absolute monarchy of the stage led to insurgency among the less timid people of London. It was one of Garrick's failings that he wished to put on only the old plays that had been tried out many times and were sure to succeed. He shunned anything new and was far more interested in cutting plays down to fit his size rather than attempting to grow in stature to fit the play.

Goldsmith wrote: "Our poet's performance must undergo a process truly chemical before it is presented to the public. It must be tried in the manager's fire; strained through a licenser, suffer from repeated corrections, till it may be a mere *caput mortuum* when it arrives before the public. . . . Getting a play on even in three or four years is a privilege reserved only for the happy few who have the arts of courting the manager as well as the muse; who have the adulation to please his vanity, powerful patrons to support their merit, or money to indemnify disappointment. I have no particular spleen against the fellow who sweeps the stage with his besom, or the hero who brushes it with his train. It were a matter of indifference to me whether our

[77]

heroines are in keeping, or our candle-snuffers burn their fingers, did not such make a great part of public care and polite conversation. Our actors assume all that state off the stage which they do on it; and to use an expression borrowed from the green-room, every one is *up* in his part. I am sorry to say it, they seem to forget their true characters."

Garrick was furious. He took the remarks as a personal affront to himself. What did this upstart mean by such utterances? In vain did Goldsmith protest that he was not dealing in personalities. Garrick refused to be mollified. Thereafter Goldsmith and Garrick were enemies. But it was one of the traits of Goldsmith that no one could remain his enemy long. Eventually they became friends again. In fact *She Stoops to Conquer* published years later in 1773 has fittingly a prologue written by David Garrick.

8

In 1760 Goldsmith met Dr. Samuel Johnson and thereafter they became the greatest of friends. Hand in hand they walk down through the pages of history and through Boswell's famous biography. Dr. Johnson was a trifle jealous of Goldsmith despite their friendship and it is largely through his disparaging utterances that Goldsmith has acquired the undeserved reputation of being a dullard. No two men could have been such poles apart as the ponderous melancholy Johnson and the small carefree Goldsmith. Yet they had two things in common.

They had both known the most abject poverty and they were both ugly enough to be gargoyles. It is interesting to note that Sir Joshua Reynolds painted the portraits of both these eccentric doctors, the two ugliest men in all literature, Reynolds who loved beauty so much, Reynolds who became immortal because of his lovely pictures of Sarah Siddons. The anatomy of ugliness is an interesting topic to muse over. Can it be possible that Reynolds saw beneath the veneer of ugliness? Can it be possible that he was able to visualize the sterling qualities possessed by these two monstrosities of men? Why was so great an artist attracted to them? And in like manner what prompted James Boswell to worship at the shrine of a man so ugly as Johnson? Could he possibly have known how great was the biography he was writing? Great men inspire great acts. Many people believe that Boswell, the biographer, was a greater man than Johnson, the subject. Perhaps Boswell wrote his book with his tongue in Johnson's cheek.

Often Goldsmith and Johnson met at the shop of Davies, the bookseller, which was a sort of literary club. Davies was the biographer of Garrick and Garrick was one of Johnson's closest friends. Davies had once been an actor but he had retired because he was too small in size to play in the great tragedies he assailed.

Davies will always be remembered because of the charmed circle in which he moved and as the inspiration of so many men of letters.

During this period Goldsmith collected a series of Chi-

[79]

nese letters originally written for the "Public Ledger" published daily by Francis Newberry. These letters were printed under the pseudonym of Lien Chi Altangi. They were supposed to be the written impressions of a native of Honan in China on a visit to London. He wrote one hundred and twenty-seven such letters. In book form the letters were called, *Citizen of the World.*

In commenting on these letters, one essayist has written: "He wanted to be a philosopher, a sort of second Confucius. Most of his acquaintances found him only confusing."

Nevertheless scattered throughout the vast material that has been written about Goldsmith, occasionally there is a brief mention of a time when Goldsmith outshone everyone present by his wit and quickness in turning a clever sentence. Personally it is my belief that he was not as dull a conversationalist as he was reputed to be. No man could write with such wit and only talk half-witted. This is merely another one of the curious legends that spring up about great people. The fault, if fault there was, was with the listeners. Listening is almost as fine an art as speaking. Goldsmith's appearance was against him, ill-featured, pock-marked, short and squat. His head was too large. He did not look brilliant, so his audience listened to him expecting him not to be brilliant. They paid little heed to what he said, searching only for faults in his diction, and pouncing on them like the tasty morsels they were.

SIR JOSHUA REYNOLDS

JUNIUS BRUTUS BOOTH AS RICHARD III

9

Johnson was fond of showering Goldsmith with advice. He was well aware of Goldsmith's many faults but he was also aware of his many virtues.

James Boswell has related how one morning Johnson received a message from Goldsmith stating that he was in great distress. He was about to be evicted by his landlady. Johnson sent him a guinea at once and later in the day he went to Goldsmith's lodgings. He had been arrested for non-payment of rent and was very angry. However with the guinea he had purchased a bottle of Madeira so that he could drown the sorrows of earth as pleasantly as possible.

Goldsmith explained to Johnson that he had a novel ready for the press. Thereupon Johnson took it to the printer, Francis Newberry, and sold it outright for £60 which he considered a fair price for it. The novel was *The Vicar of Wakefield.* Newberry thought so little of the manuscript that he kept it for two years before he had the courage to publish it.

It was during this period that Goldsmith finished *The Traveller,* the poem on which he had been working for years. Samuel Johnson contributed a few lines to it and it was largely through the influence of the famed Doctor that Goldsmith was stimulated sufficiently to get it ready for publication. It was published by Newberry December 19th 1764. An interesting fact in connection with

[81]

it is that it was the first literary effort to which Goldsmith affixed his own name.

Immediately Goldsmith became famous. He did not become famous over-night like Byron but he became famous over many, many nights of toil and ceaseless effort.

The poem went through edition after edition and made a great deal of money for Newberry but all Goldsmith ever received for it was twenty pounds.

The Vicar of Wakefield was published in 1766. Two months later it went into a second printing and never since that time has it been out of print. It should not have been called *The Vicar of Wakefield* but *The Vicar of the World* for there is no country in which it has not been published. This is not a novel for any one country or for any single creed. It's appeal is universal, since it has as its theme the love of home and quietude, coupled with a sly and gentle humor. Washington Irving, greatest of Goldsmith's biographers, points out how odd it is that the supreme novel extant of happy married life should have been written by a bachelor.

That same year Goldsmith decided to try his hand at drama. He decided to write a comedy entitled *The Good-Natured Man*. Certainly he was amply fitted for such an assignment. He worked on it whenever his other literary work would permit.

It was finally completed in 1767. It had been intended for Covent Garden but that theatre was in a bad way owing to the death of Rich, the manager. Garrick was the logical person to turn to but the feud between Goldsmith and Garrick still continued. However, Goldsmith had now earned for himself an enviable place in the literary world so Garrick was not adverse to declaring an armistice. This was accomplished through the friendly offices of Sir Joshua Reynolds who brought the two together in his house in Leicester Square. Nevertheless Garrick could not help acting the part of Emperor of the Drama and there ensued much delay over the presentation of the play. Fortunately, at this time, Colman, a rival manager took over the affairs of Covent Garden. Goldsmith at once got in touch with him and the play was immediately accepted. The following day Goldsmith wrote to Garrick informing him that rights to *The Good-Natured Man* had been disposed of. Although Garrick's reply was cultured and dignified, he must have written it with considerable chagrin.

Garrick was so disgruntled that he used every device in his power to make Goldsmith's road a difficult one. He purchased a play written by Hugh Kelly, one of Goldsmith's chums. It was a comedy entitled *False Delicacy*. At once Garrick ballyhooed the play to the sky although it possessed little merit. Garrick urged Colman to hold back the production of *The Good-Natured Man* until *False Delicacy* had run its course. Colman and Garrick had been at sword's points but when Colman agreed to the delay, a pseudo-friendship was patched up between them.

False Delicacy opened in Drury Lane January 23rd

[83]

1768. The opening night was undoubtedly mostly paper. The audience paid for their admission with applause. Nor were they niggardly in this respect. Garrick knew all the tricks of the trade. It was not hard for him to get journalists to write eulogies about it. *False Delicacy* was a great success. The applause was great but no echo of the play still remains. Nobody today even knows what the play was about. But *The Good-Natured Man,* though it disappointed all Goldsmith's friends when it opened, so lukewarm was its reception, is known wherever the English language is spoken.

The lack of enthusiasm on the part of the audience was a considerable blow to Goldsmith. He was utterly miserable. Nevertheless he tried to assume an air of nonchalance he was far from feeling.

Despite this, he received greater financial return from *The Good-Natured Man* than he had for any other literary work. The exact amount was £500. Immediately he moved to better rooms and fitted them out lavishly at a cost of £400. The other hundred pounds I daresay he used up dodging bailiffs and creditors. Or perhaps in his fine new rooms he gave a dinner for them. There is, I believe, no record of his ever attempting to pay back any of his vast debts. He always believed that his greatest asset was his power to borrow, nor did he see any reason to turn this great asset into a liability by returning any of the money.

10

When I started writing about Goldsmith all that I meant to set down were a few remarks about *She Stoops to Conquer,* for after all "the play's the thing." But in the case of Goldsmith his life was as interesting as the play.

She Stoops to Conquer was produced by Colman at Covent Garden in 1773. But Colman was very doubtful of its success. It was his belief that it might not last even through a second performance. It is odd but true that no matter what Goldsmith attempted, his efforts were met by a total lack of enthusiasm. Those who walked with him and met him every day were too close to appreciate his stature. The body of a pygmy, the mind of a giant.

Months had gone by during the play's negotiations and had it not been once more for the kindly efforts of Doctor Johnson, Colman might never have made up his mind. He thought the play had a bad plot, that it lacked a sustaining interest. Little did he dream that its plot was sufficiently interesting to sustain it on the boards continuously for more than a century and a half. Incidentally it should be added that the title was not decided upon until the play had long been in rehearsal. Many names were suggested. Finally it was decided to call it *The Mistakes of a Night.* At the last minute, Goldsmith prefixed the words to it, *She Stoops to Conquer* and so it has been called ever since.

The play was founded on a true incident that occurred

[85]

during the time he attended school at Edgeworthstown. Leaving Lissoy on a borrowed horse to return to school, with only a pound in his pocket, he had arrived at Ardagh at dusk. He had assumed a cloak of insolence to hide his embarrassment for he was only about sixteen at the time, an awkward hobbledehoy.

Stopping a man on the road he demanded to be directed to the best house in town. Now this house was owned by a rich squire named Featherstone and when the feather-brained boy stormed in and started ordering him about as though he had been a lackey, he bowed servilely, hiding his smile, nor did he bother telling Goldsmith he was in a private home. Not till morning did Oliver discover how he had blundered for when he asked for his bill, Squire Featherstone laughed and waved him aside, explaining the excellence of the joke. I daresay Goldsmith was quite happy to play the fool once again inasmuch as he thereby saved money he could ill-afford to spend. Upon this incident he built up his comedy.

I might add that the Squire's comely daughter was a party to the hoax and derived great pleasure from the droll incident, especially when Goldsmith had made a magnificent gesture and invited the wife and daughter of the innkeeper to share his food with him.

11

The opening night of *She Stoops to Conquer* finally came. Goldsmith was so overwrought over the service his

friends had done him in helping to get the play produced that he felt they would be greatly humiliated if
the play should prove a failure. So when it was time to
raise the curtain on the first act, he rushed out and
walked down to the river. He was ready to jump in and
drown himself if the play did not succeed. But at the end
of the second act, one of his friends rushed out to him
and said, "Come to the theatre. Oliver, the play is a
great success!"

And it was.

12

Goldsmith's death occurred on April 4th 1774.

There is a memorial to him in the Poet's Corner of
Westminster Abbey and there is a statue by Foley at the
Gateway of Trinity College, Dublin. But his greatest
memorial is that he is still remembered through the ages.
His books are still read. His plays continue.

With his pen, he had a magical touch. He did not
write with ink but with enchantment. He wrote easily,
without conscious effort, his characters were real people.
He enjoyed writing. Therein lay his charm.

When Goldsmith died he was £2000 in debt; but the
debt which the world owes to him is inestimable.

6

GLIMPSES OF EDWIN BOOTH

1

IN THE middle Eighties Edwin Booth purchased a charming house in Boston, an old-fashioned residence on Chestnut Street within a short block of Beacon Street. Chestnut Street was at the time well-mannered, expansive; an aristocrat among streets, proud of its heritage, trying to live down the fact that the lower part of it was in a slightly lower social stratum. Frequently this section was called Horsechestnut Street in tribute to the many private stables that adorned it.

The house was of brick with an elaborate front and windows of purple glass. Most of the genteel houses had blue window panes, but purple glass was considered a trifle more "utterly utter." Royal purple it was in winter time when the snow fell like ermine trimmings upon the window ledges. This was the age of over-stuffed rooms. No house was well-furnished unless it was so crowded with furniture, lamps and bric-a-brac that it required the skill of a clever navigator to make a tour of the room without knocking over a whatnot cabinet or tripping over a tiger-skin rug, with the tiger's head still adorning it, its glaring artificial eyes and competent-looking teeth seemingly waiting for a choice mouthful of any one so foolhardy as to stray within biting distance.

A bronze bust of Booth adorned the hall. His personal rooms were on the ground floor. Those of his daughter Edwina were on the floor above where she used to hold afternoon receptions which were well-attended and very successful. The tea she served was of the finest. So, too, were the cake and cookies. Edwina was an admirable hostess, both gracious and graceful. Her father adored her and she had great power over him.

The social position of an actor in Boston, at that time, was very high, as though the city wished to swing away from its early puritanism. And the Booths were honored and respected by everyone. Edwin Booth in private life was distinguished by simplicity, a total disregard of ostentation, thereby showing his greatness. There never was anything theatrical about him either on or off the stage, despite the fact that he was a born actor. He who is to the manner born finds little necessity to put on an over-emphasized parade of manners. Edwin had a delightful habit of illustrating with expression and gesture the matter about which he was talking. No more forceful form of emphasis could be devised. He was always genial and cordial despite his natural reserve.

2

William Stuart, one of the earliest managers under whom Edwin Booth appeared, often used to tell about a polyglot performance for which he was responsible.

"It was Othello," he said, "and Davison, the great tragedian played Othello in German, Edwin Booth played Iago in English and Methea Schiller played Desdemona in German and English as the dialogue was directed to either Davison or Booth. I paid Davison one thousand dollars each for three performances. He subsequently was eager to play for five hundred dollars, then for two hundred and fifty, and on departing, like most of these great German tragedians, he would have recited a soliloquy on the clock for ten dollars. He shortly after, as might be expected, went mad, and Schiller, poor girl, died of cholera at Pittsburgh on the same day as her husband and two children were on their way East from Salt Lake City."

Mr. Stuart was the manager of the Winter Garden Theatre when Edwin Booth played his first engagement there in about 1857.

3

Edwin Booth and Madame Ristori acted *Macbeth* in the New York Academy of Music on May 7th 1885. Madame Ristori was then in her sixtieth year and was making her farewell tour of the American Stage.

The house was crowded. Over three thousand people witnessed the performance. Many of the ultra-fashionable set, to whom money meant absolutely nothing, paid as high as five dollars each for seats. The scenery, however, was of the poorest. The management used stock sets that had been knocking around the city for years. Supers had been mustered at the last minute at one dollar each. They didn't know whether they were employed to be soldiers or clowns and apparently they didn't care, nor did the audience who had come solely to see Booth and Ristori. They would have applauded if there had been no other actors at all. The witch's cauldron was fit for burlesque, nor could it stir up much of a broth. The soldiers looked as though they were afraid of the scene-shifters who appeared on the stage from time to time as if in an effort to frighten them. Nor were they embarrassed by the fact that Shakespeare had neglected to write any part for them. And to cap the climax a small cat walked across the stage and yawned in open defiance, as though to proclaim the fact that he refused to be awed.

But when Ristori and Booth were on the stage, as though by magic all the inefficiencies due to managerial laxity were swept away, leaving in their wake, eloquent silence and rapt attention. No longer was the witch's cauldron needed; here were wizardry and witchery, voices that spoke words that spun themselves into a web of fine gold that spread itself out over the audience. Those who saw that performance, never forgot it. They repeated stories in praise so frequently that they became legends. And oddly enough, in the retelling, the scenery became pageants of beauty, the soldiers became an army of splendid strength, and the little cat disappeared from the accounts entirely as though he had never pattered across the stage on his soft little feet, nor given vent to that magnificent yawn.

4

The marriage of Edwina Booth and Edward Grossman took place at the Booth home in Boston on the afternoon of May 17th 1885, in a veritable maze of palms and flowers. The home was turned into a garden for the occasion. The ceremony which took place in one of the upper rooms was performed by the Rev. Dr. A. Bartol. Mr. William Warren, a close friend, was the only member of the theatrical profession present.

5

On September 10th 1886, a former chum of Edwin's who lived in Charleston, South Carolina, received a check from him for one thousand dollars, accompanied by the following letter:

"The earthquake horror reminds me that I have (or had) many dear friends in Charleston. I can't help all of 'em, but if the enclosed can relieve you and the dear ones, use it—would to God I could offer more. Bad as it is, it might be worse. The Almighty loves us, despite his chastisements. Be true to him. He will not desert you. My life has been a chapter of tragedies, as you know, but I have never despaired—never lost my 'grip' of the 'eternal truth'. The worst is not so long that we can say, this is the worst. Give my love to all old friends of mine, and assure them that though I may never see them again in the flesh, they are vivid in my memory, 'wreathed with roses and red ribbons'. Your old friend, Ned."

6

According to the "Buffalo Times," once during the days of Edwin Booth's early struggles, he was barnstorming down in Virginia at a place called, Lee's Landing. The improvised theatre was a tobacco warehouse and it was crowded by the planters from miles around. Booth and his companions had arranged to take the weekly steamer, expected to call late at night, and between the acts they were busy packing up. The play was *The Merchant of Venice,* and they were just going on for the trial scene when they heard a whistle; and the manager came running in to say the steamer had arrived, and would leave again in ten minutes. As that was their only chance for a week of getting away, they were in a terrible quandary.

"If we explain matters," said the manager, "they will think they are being cheated, and we will have a free fight."

Edwin was Bassanio and resolved to rely on the ignorance of the Virginians of those days to pull him through all right. So when old George Ruggles—who was doing Shylock—began to sharpen his knife on his boots, Booth walked straight up to him and solemnly said, "You are bound to have the flesh, are you?"

"You bet your life!" said Ruggles.

"Now, I'll make you one more offer," continued Booth, "in addition to this big bag of ducats, I'll throw in two kegs of nigger-head terback, a shot-gun and two of the best coon-dogs in the state."

"I'm blamed if I don't do it!" responded Shylock, much to the approbation of the audience, who were tobacco-raisers and coon-hunters to a man.

[93]

"And to show that there's no ill-feeling," put in Portia, "we'll wind up with a Virginia reel."

When they got on board the steamer, the captain, who had witnessed the conclusion of the play, remarked: "I'd like to see the whole of that play some time, gentlemen. I'm blamed if I thought that fellow Shakespeare had so much snap in him."

7

Edwin Thomas Booth cast his first, and the only vote of his life, for Abraham Lincoln in the autumn of 1864. On the night of April 14th 1865 Booth was in Boston, acting the part of Sir Edward Mortimer. He had just arrived from New York where he had triumphantly acted the part of Hamlet for one hundred nights, the record for the time. A committee of representative citizens had called upon him on the last night to acquaint him with the fact that they had ordered a medal to be struck in his honor, commemorating the event. Truly it seemed that the good omens connected with his birth had all come true, for when he had been born at Booth Farm, Hartford City, Maryland on November 13th 1833, the night had been remarkable. The sky was illuminated to dawn-brilliance by a meteoric shower. Superstitious folk, and there were many, predicted that his path through life, in like manner, would be meteoric.

On the morning of April 15th 1865, Edwin Booth awakened into a world that no longer existed for him. Abraham Lincoln had been assassinated by the hand of John Wilkes Booth, his brother. Edwin left Boston that

[94]

night and repaired to his home in New York. Devoted friends rallied to his side, endeavoring to show in what personal esteem he was universally held. But he was overcome with grief and shame. The meteor had fallen. Now he would probably have to give up the stage. During the months that followed, his health broke. He had had enough of life. It had defeated him. Gone was the sun. He was walking through a valley of shadow that seemed without end. But finally at the insistence of those closest to him, he roused from his lethargy and clutched once more at life. He returned to the stage at the Garden Theatre in *Hamlet* on January 3rd 1866. Immense crowds welcomed him, many coming from other cities, Philadelphia, Baltimore, Boston and even Washington. The house was sold out. Perhaps never before or since has an actor received a more perfect tribute. The moment he stepped out on the stage, he was applauded and cheered. And the play was halted for fully fifteen minutes. Thereafter, wherever he appeared, he was greeted in like manner. It was as though the vast crowds wished him to know that he had their devotion and sympathy.

Nevertheless it was nineteen years before Booth ever played in Washington, D. C., again. The nearest he ever came to it was Baltimore, and whenever he appeared in Baltimore special trains brought his admirers in throngs from the Capitol City. Then he yielded to the insistence of a Washington manager and appeared there once more during February 1884.

To me there is no more tragic figure in this greatest

[95]

of American tragedies, than Mrs. Junius Brutus Booth, the mother of both John Wilkes and Edwin. What must her feelings have been when news of the assassination was brought to her? What were her thoughts through all the years that followed until her death? Thankful she must have been that her husband had died in 1852. Something of her sorrow is reflected in a book by her daughter Asia Booth Clarke, written in September 1865. It was called, *Passages, Incidents and Anecdotes, in the Life of Junius Brutus Booth By His Daughter.*" The book begins thus: "A calamity without precedent has fallen on our country. We, of all families, secure in domestic love and retirement, are stricken desolate!"

The book has this tragic dedication:

"MOTHER:
*that name, so Hallowed and
Revered, is but a synonym of sorrow;
To you
The very patient and long suffering,
I dedicate these pages.*"

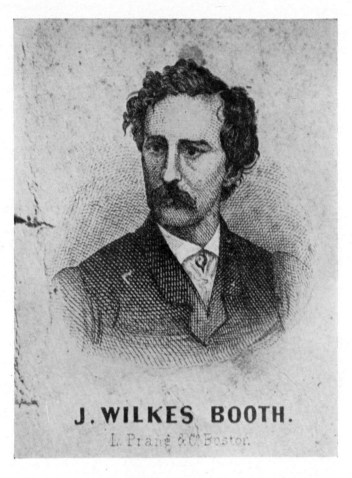

JOHN WILKES BOOTH

DION BOUCICAULT

7

DION BOUCICAULT

1

TODAY WHEN I was going over some old letters, I came across one from A. M. Palmer. It was dated, New York, September 19th, 1890, and read as follows: "I am requested to ask you to serve as one of the pall bearers at the funeral of the late Dion Boucicault on Monday next, September 22nd. The funeral will take place from the Church of the Transfiguration, East 29th Street at 10 o'clock on the forenoon of that day. Pall bearers will meet at 103 West Fifty-fifth Street at 9:15. Please address reply to me at the Madison Square Theatre."

What memories that letter brings back to me, for Dion Boucicault was one of the most brilliant men I have ever met. He was the author of over three hundred plays, many of which were adaptations, during his career of half a century on the stage. When he was connected with Wallack's Theatre, he would stop at Brentano's Bookstore which was then at Broadway and Eighth Street, buy a special book and in a week he would have it dramatized. He used to come to my theatre with his young wife, listen to the first act of a play, then he would retire to the smoking-room. He did not care to see any more of the play. He was able to tell from the first act what the entire play was about. In this respect he was almost clairvoyant for he seldom guessed wrong. He cared nothing for acting if it were good. If it were bad, he pondered over it, as a doctor might puzzle over an ailing patient.

2

Dion Boucicault was born in Dublin, Ireland, December 20th 1822, of Irish-French parentage. He was educated in Dublin and at London University. He became a dramatist at the age of nineteen, in 1841, when he wrote his first play, *London Assurance* which was shown in Covent Garden Theatre in March of the same year. On this play he gave the author's name as "Lee Morton," perhaps due to timidity on his part. He didn't want to be ridiculed by his friends if it failed. His caution, however, was unnecessary for the play met with wild acclaim. In February of the following year, he wrote *The Irish Heiress*. It was a dismal failure. In September 1842, at the Haymarket Theatre, was presented *Alma Mater; or a Cure for Coquettes,* "by Dion Boucicault" for now he had sufficient confidence in himself to use his own name. It was excellently received. Then followed a long series of plays, most of which were successes. Many are of the opinion that his greatest play was *Colleen Bawn* which he wrote in 1860. Others still talk about *The Shaughraun* in which he played the leading part, for Boucicault became an actor at the age of thirty and thereafter divided his time between acting and writing. Another of his more celebrated works was his version of *Rip Van Winkle* which he wrote for Joseph Jefferson.

[98]

bly no play had a more distinguished lineage than
e for it was suggested by an old German folk tale
n the Harz Mountains, its origin lost in the mists of
centuries. It was then called, *Carl the Shepherd.*
n Washington Irving re-wrote it and gave it univer-
s. appeal, changing the name of the hero and choosing
the Catskill Mountains as a locale. Later it was made into
a play several times and many versions were acted. Dion
Boucicault rewrote all these old plays and devised a more
lovable hero than any of the others. After this, Joseph
Jefferson went over the play again and imbued it with
his own individuality. The rest is theatrical history.

3

On January 18th 1936, I received the following letter,
which I am quoting in full because I found it so interesting:

"Dear Mr. Frohman: I see by the papers you are writing a book. I have known and interviewed many celebrities. In 1875 I was with Mr. Dion Boucicault and
remained with him until 1885. In 1883 he sent me to
England to run his house, 16 New Burlington Street,
London, as a private hotel. I had Miss Mary Anderson
stay there six months when she played *Ingomar* at the Lyceum Theatre, London. She had Tennyson, Longfellow,
James Russell Lowell and Cardinal Newman to visit her.
She gave me a part in *A Winter's Tale.* In 1885, I had an
apartment in Oxford Mansions which I let on a sublease
to Lillian Russell. In 1886 I was with Mr. Lawrence Bar-

rett. I went on tour with him. After I left his employ I was outside representative for Mr. Falk, the photographer in the old Flatiron Building in New York. During the time I was with him I got Thomas Edison, President Cleveland, Jay Gould, and Rider Haggard to let him take their pictures. I could tell you many interesting things. I have a letter from Mr. Boucicault written on Madison Square Theatre paper when he had his dramatic classes there. Mr. Brentano, the publisher, was my friend for over fifty years. I would be pleased to hear from you if you are interested. Yours truly,

Robert Gaul."

I smiled as I read the letter, and I wondered how many stories of famous people still could be gathered from those who knew them, stories that unfortunately never find their way into print. Mr. Gaul had said he would be glad to hear from me, if I was interested. Of course I was interested. Who wouldn't be? This was a voice from the past.

So at once I wrote to Mr. Gaul, suggesting that he write a few pages about himself, especially about the time when he was with Boucicault. He replied at once, and thus I am able to give here a few pages from the unpublished, *Memoirs of Robert Gaul.*

"I was born in Ipswich, Suffolk, England, April 12th, 1855. My father was an engineer. My uncle, Alfred Gaul, was a celebrated composer. His best-known composition was *The Holy City*. Ipswich is famous for "The White Horse Tavern," mentioned in *Pickwick Papers* and a the birthplace of Cardinal Wolsey, and because it was here that David Garrick commenced his career as an actor.

"When I was a boy, my father had my head examined by a traveling phrenologist who said that I had no mechanical ideas. He said it would be better if I got a position where I could travel and see the world. So I went to London when I was sixteen and secured a position as page and buttons with Captain Maxsie, the hero of George Meredith's, *Beachamp's Career*. On one occasion he gave a dinner at which were Darwin, Herbert Spencer, John Stuart Mill, Braglouch and George Meredith. The Captain's wife was a very beautiful woman and her picture is in the Metropolitan Museum of Art in New York under the title of *Phryne*. About a year later I went on board Lord Londonderry's yacht as steward. He gave a dinner one night to the Prince of Wales, later King Edward VII, and among the guests were the Duke of Rutland, Winston Churchill, and Lord Brassy. We were lying off Cowes, Isle of Wight, in a rough sea. The yacht was rolling. I was serving the soup, and as the ship lurched, I upset it down Londonderry's back. He called out to the chief steward, 'Put that boy off my boat at once!' The Prince of Wales said, 'Londonderry, quite an accident. Why don't you let the boy stay?' But Londonderry over-rode the Prince and my nautical career was at an end.

"I was very dejected after this and decided to come to America. I sailed on the *Britannic* of the White Star

[101]

Line and arrived in New York on the Fourth of July
1874. I walked up Broadway and happened to go in the
Broadway Central Hotel which had gained notoriety due
to the fact that it was here that Jim Fiske was shot by
Stokes. I told the clerk at the desk that I was searching
for a position. He spoke to the manager about me. As a
result I was placed in charge of one of the parlors which
ran the entire width of the hotel on the first floor. During the time I was there I became friendly with Buffalo
Bill who stopped at the Broadway Central when he was
in town.

"Jeffreys Lewis who played in *The Shaughraun* was
stopping at the Hotel. She became interested in me. She
made an appointment for me to see Dion Boucicault. I
met him at the St. James Hotel. He was writing a play
at the time that I knocked at the door of his room. He
called out, 'Come in.' I entered the room and stood
inside the door. He was busy and I did not interrupt
him. For about ten minutes I stood there, making no
sound. Finally he looked up and said, 'Oh, you're the
young man who is looking for a position.' I told him I
was. He asked me what wages I wanted. I asked for thirty
dollars per month. He read my references, then he said,
'Young man, I'll give you fifty.' Thereafter for ten years
I worked with Boucicault and never have I met anyone
more liberal. For instance on one occasion he said to me,
'Robert, I am going to write a paper for you.' It was a
paper about the size of the tabloids today, although only
a few pages, and was illustrated by scenes from *The*

Shaughraun, together with little stories and jokes that he had written or collected. The entire proceeds from this work went to me. I used to have boys sell the paper in the Grand Opera House on 23rd Street during the intermissions of the show. Boucicault used to receive his salary and royalty every night when the show was over. And I went down to Morgan's Bank in Wall Street every morning to deposit it for him.

"Although I went with Boucicault as his dresser, he used to call me his confidential man and whenever we went to hotels he always paid my bill as a guest. He usually dined in his suite while I dined in the main dining-room downstairs. When Boucicault gave up his rooms at the St. James Hotel, he moved to Pinard's, the celebrated caterer, who had just built a new house on 15th Street. Boucicault occupied the entire second floor and furnished the rooms himself in luxurious manner. I believe he was one of the first persons in New York to have a tiled bathroom. The walls were imported Minton china and all the bathroom fixtures were of sterling silver. In the front room there was a log fireplace. On each side of the mantelpiece was a pedestal on which stood a bronze figure. One was Aphrodite, the other Diana, and each held a lamp. The windows were stained glass. As you entered the rooms there was a magnificent Bengal tiger rug on the floor over an antique Persian carpet. Facing the mantelpiece was a very long bookcase, above which was a panel picture of Balzac's *Comedie Humaine.* All Boucicault's manuscripts were in various compartments of the bookcase, the small panels of which were paintings on leather, scenes from Shakespeare.

"The apartment consisted of two large rooms, bath-room and trunkroom. All meals were sent up by Pinard. Between the two main rooms were a series of cupboards, one of which was in the form of an ice-box, another was a wine cabinet and the third was a place to keep logs. While no cooking was done in the apartment, he usually kept the ice-box well-stocked with food in case he took anyone home with him after the play.

"One morning Boucicault came to me and brought me a bag filled with letters. He said, 'Now, Robert, you can tear those letters up and throw them in the waste-basket.' I read many of the letters before destroying them. Had I known what I know today, I'd have kept them, for now they would be worth a great deal of money. There were letters from Tennyson, Longfellow, Charles Dickens, Disraeli, Charles Reade, Parnell, Victor Hugo, Ouida and many celebrated people.

"Boucicault entertained a good deal. He once gave a dinner to Gilbert and Sullivan at Pinard's. Among the guests were Delancy Kane, Thorndike Rice, then editor of 'The North American Review,' Dana of the Sun, Les-ter Wallack and John McCullough.

"On one occasion while Dion Boucicault was putting on a stiff front shirt, which in those days had to be put on over the head, he became angry and said to me, 'Get me a razor.' I did so. Thereupon he slit the shirt down the front so that it could be put on like a coat. The next morning he sent me to Hutchinson, the Haberdasher, who had a store on the present site of the Flatiron Building, to order three dozen shirts opening in front with buttons. This was the origin of the open-front shirt."

Here Robert Gaul's memoirs end. I wish they were longer for they bring back memories of the days when we were very young, days which we old-timers will never forget.

8

SCISSORS AND PASTE

1. *The Theatre Magazine*

I HAVE heard it said that many authors write their books with scissors and paste and so perhaps I may be excused for writing one chapter of this book in like manner. The scissors needs sharpening, the paste doesn't stick but there is nothing wrong with the source of my inspiration—the files of *The Theatre Magazine* from March 1886 to June 1890. Interspersed with the quotations are a few of my own observations which I hope will not be out of place.

The magazine was edited by Deshler Welch. How ably he handled his job is suggested by the following clipping from the *Pittsburgh Bulletin:* "The Holliday Number of *The Theatre* was a pretty publication—a Deshler Welch rarebit, deviled, in a shell of terra cotta and blue."

2. *First Appearance of Joseph Jefferson*

Of Joseph Jefferson's first appearance on the stage, when fourteen, Mr. L. C. Davis gives a touching description. The young actor's widowed mother had for weeks trained him in the music, words, and business of his part. They were very poor, and both hoped intensely that the début would be successful. The night came, and young

Jefferson took his place upon the stage more dead than alive with fright. He became conscious that his mother was watching him, and, though half-blinded with fear, he saw her hands tremble up to her mouth, saw the tears filling her eyes, and saw her trying to smile encouragement to him through them; yet after the first line or two, he broke down utterly, and, amid a storm of hisses, he tottered off at the wing, to which his mother was clinging for support, so great was her distress. He flung himself into her arms, crying out through his sobs and hers that he had failed—that he should never succeed. The lovely lady and loving mother died, not, indeed, before her son had gained a good position upon the stage, but before he had reached the success that would have made her so proud and happy. (*May 17th 1886*)

3. *Mark Twain*

In *The Theatre Magazine* dated May 31st, 1886, appeared the following paragraph: "Mark Twain is a humorist, as everybody knows. But everybody does not know what a clever, sagacious, hard-headed man of business he is. He will soon be one of the richest publishers in America, and he seldom makes a blunder in trade. It may be taken for granted, therefore, that, when he gave Mr. Daniel Frohman $1,000 *not* to produce his new play, *The American Claimant* (written in collaboration with Mr. Howells), he displayed extraordinary forethought. He came to the conclusion that, since he could not stand his own play, the public would not be likely to stand it."

. . . .

The American Claimant was written for Mr. A. E. Burback who was a humorous lecturer. He was desirous of adopting the stage as a profession. Twain and Howells organized a company to produce the play and they wished me to present it to the public, which I was quite willing to do. They entered into an agreement to reimburse me for any losses I might sustain. All profits were to be divided between us.

The play was about a scientist who had invented a machine that would instantly put out any fire, no matter how large it might be. He made his first appearance in the play through a second-story window of a house. He was carrying the machine on his back. As he entered he set fire to the place and even though he had the machine with him, he couldn't put it out. This was the only funny scene in the entire play. It was a failure and it drew no audience. A week passed and I did not receive any money from the firm to indemnify me for my losses so I said to Mark Twain: "If your company does not pay me for my losses on this play I will keep it on."

Whereupon he instantly hustled around and made up with his colleagues the required sum and so the play was stopped. However another story of his, *The Prince and the Pauper* which was made into a play for me was a great success.

4. *Approval*

Coming out of the theatre the other night, after the impressive performance of Booth's *Hamlet,* attention was drawn to the effusive delight of a young lady who was thus trying apparently to show her gratitude to the gentleman upon whose arm she was resting: "I've had a real good time, George," said she, "and it's a lovely play. It's so full of quotations." (*June 7th 1886*)

5. *Sarah Bernhardt*

Sarah Bernhardt is writing a play. When she gets tired she uses herself for a book-mark and hides between the pages of her manuscript. (*June 7th 1886*)

6. *Realism in Acting*

Betterton, when playing *Hamlet,* it is said, always turned pale on the appearance of the ghost.

In one of the ranting scenes, the blood rushed to Forrest's face, while the veins in his neck would swell up and stand out like whip cords.

Mrs. Siddons found no difficulty in shedding tears when there was an appropriate time for them.

Garrick's performance of *Richard the Third,* had enough in reality to convince many that he imagined, for a time, that he actually was the crooked-backed king, and possessed all his feelings. Somebody happened to mention this in Johnson's presence, when the latter replied: "If that is the case, he ought to be hanged every time he plays it." (*August 30th 1886*)

7. *General Sherman*

Now that General Sherman is making his home in New York City—this will be his permanent abode hereafter—the list of conspicuous first-nighters will undoubtedly be increased. General Sherman likes a good play almost as much as a pretty girl. There are more pretty girls than good plays in this neighborhood but the fact will not prevent him from taking his chances now and then with the rest of us. (*Sept. 20th 1886.*)

General Sherman was a great friend of Edwin Booth. He often appeared at "The Players' Club" where he met many actors of note and where he was always a welcome guest.

8. *The Real Hamlet*

An old-time friend of Mr. Edwin Booth, speaking of the tragedian, said: "His nature is the most unique of any man in public life. His indifference to money, society and the things which the world ranks as pleasure is absolute and definite. Few understand him and he tries not to be understood. He is really the *Hamlet* of the nineteenth century—the melancholy dreamer of the Western World." (*Sept. 27th 1886*)

9. *And More Hamlet*

Mr. Lawrence Barrett recently said to the editor of the *Louisville Times:* "I don't know what is to happen when Mr. Booth dies. I do not see a single gleam of promise in the skies for the elevation and ennobling of the stage. It is rapidly falling into the hands of common, vulgar people who are as incapable of playing the great parts which the dramatic geniuses of England and America have kept aloft for two hundred years as was the Gravedigger of personating Hamlet. The cardinal trouble with the younger men of the American stage is their lack of application, their contempt for industry. Most of them come to the stage ill-prepared, and lack the strength and the impulse to overcome their deficiencies. Genius itself must labor to accomplish great ends, and how much more, then, must mere talent exert itself. Year after year, you see fellows who have gained a little notoriety by playing in melodrama, or mayhap rough-and-tumble farces, or who may have supported an eminent actor, and thus shared some of his lustre, starting out to attempt the great characters made sacred by tradition. In one place a man who was *Harlequin* to-day essays *Benedict* or *Jacques* to-morrow, and in another the man who was a heavy villain yesterday starts out to star as *Hamlet* or *Iago*. Crop after crop of these aspirants are withered by the frost of failure, but they seem to have plenty of successors, undeterred by the fate of those who have gone before." (*Nov. 8th 1886*)

The best *Hamlet* after Edwin Booth was Forbes-Robertson. He lacked the emotional quality, but he had the presence and the intellectual quality. Booth's personality was unique because he could play *Romeo* one night and *Iago* the next night with equal effect, which is not cus-

[111]

tomary among actors in general, because their personalities do not permit such flexibility.

E. H. Sothern was the next best *Hamlet* because his temperament lent itself somewhat to the peculiar qualities of the character. In fact, when he played *Romeo* he was more like *Hamlet* than he was like *Romeo*.

Henry Irving had the intelligence and the mental ability to play any part even though they all did not fit his rigid personality, but he had great intellect and a wonderful dramatic temperament.

Jack Barrymore's *Hamlet* had its value for two reasons. One was his youth and the other was his dramatic intensity. The two together had a pronounced effect on his audience.

While Booth played *Hamlet* in New York for a hundred nights, Barrymore was able to exceed his record by a few nights. He afterwards played the part in London.

A story is told about a little old lady in a western town who had a good seat and was watching the performance of *Hamlet*. At the end of the second act she said to the gentleman sitting next to her, "Will you tell me who that man in black was?"

"That was *Hamlet*," was the reply.

"Oh, thank you," said the little old lady, picking up her umbrella and her bag and starting to leave the theatre.

"But," said the gentleman, "there are three more acts."

"I know," she said. "That's why I'm going."

EDWIN BOOTH AS RICHELIEU

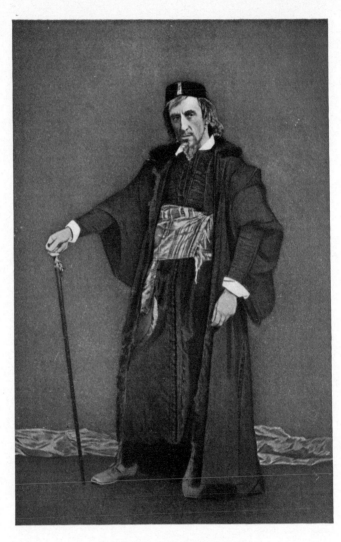

SIR HENRY IRVING AS SHYLOCK

10. *Lamb Chops*

Mr. Edwin Booth has been worried a good deal by the threat of the Lamb's Club to give him a dinner. He is understood to have said to the committee: "My God! gentlemen, if I eat I'll have dyspepsia, and if I have dyspepsia I'll make a speech, and if I make a speech I'll ruin my business for the next six months. Don't, I beseech you; don't do it! Besides, Winter will want to read a poem, and you ought to have some consideration for a man with no stomach." (*Nov. 15th 1886*)

11. *The Mad-Hatters*

There are probably women who feel mad when they realize that "all the world's a stage," because a hat can't be made big enough to obscure it. (*Nov. 22nd 1886*)

12. *Hats Off*

Mr. Daniel Frohman, the manager of the Lyceum Theatre, and a clever business man, has instituted a plan which may serve as a sort of boomerang advertisement. He asks the ladies who attend his theatre to remove their bonnets, and has arranged proper facilities for their safe keeping—that is, for the bonnets. He has appealed to Mrs. Grover Cleveland to espouse his cause, but whether that lady supports the movement as a matter which will assist the "brilliant appearance" of the audience or to render a service to a suffering class of men who are compelled to look over these bonnets, is not exactly understood. Apparently, however, Mr. Frohman has had very

[113]

little experience with women. He shows a maiden thoughtlessness in this instance which betrays a sad want of knowledge of either woman's philosophy or her soul. Mrs. Cleveland is a young girl—undeniably beautiful—but she cannot become a fashion censor in this country for reasons that are quite obvious. What she cares to do she can do because she hasn't anything else on hand just now but the upholding of presidential dignity, and living in royal state. But she forgets that this country is not Europe, and it will be an everlastingly long while before it will even take upon itself any similarity of life in its aristocratic belongings. In England the majority of the social and better class are people of leisure, ready and able to follow any convenient fashionable movement. The English theatres are not arranged like ours, and people of means—and idleness—frequent only the stalls where bonnets are forbidden. Here "the pit" is a seating place where silks and satins might jar with blue jeans, and any juxtaposition enforced will have the effect of making things decidedly objectionable, to say nothing of a positive box-office alarm. It is a difficult matter—and Mr. Frohman really ought to know about this, you know—to induce a woman to take off her bonnet when she is calling at the house of a most intimate friend. Some women take their afternoon naps in their bonnets. Surely then our young theatre manager will not presume that these evidences of female insanity can be immediately overcome by him? Another thing Mr. Frohman has never observed, most likely, and that is many women arrange

[114]

the hair to suit the bonnet, and sometimes the latter is a positive cloak for excuses, as many women look much better in their bonnets, and buy these little arrangements as the most important factor in self adornment. I know of a number of men who can testify to this by the bills which have been sent in afterwards.

Seriously the plan will never work in this country. Many women start off to the theatre in a few moments' notice. Many are in town only for a few hours, and are unprepared to go to any inconvenience simply "to add to the appearance of the house." No. If Mrs. Grover Cleveland and Mr. Frohman wish to do an act of kindness, they will organize a commission to experiment on milliners for the purpose of lowering the heighth of hats and bonnets, and Mr. Steele Mackaye will invent a plan whereby a big post and a big hat will be no obstruction. (*Dec. 13th 1886*)

In connection with the above news item, I am reminded of the gentleman who went to see a play but was unfortunate enough to sit in front of a woman with an elegant hat. In fact it was more than elegant, it was massive. He sat patiently through the first act but the scenery on her hat never changed. He began to grow bored. Leaning forward, he touched her on the shoulder,

"Madame," said he politely, "would you mind removing your hat so I can see the play?"

She smiled sweetly as she complied with his request. But as she removed her head-gear up popped a pompadour that was a vision to behold.

[115]

The gentleman apologized. "Thank you," he said, "but now would you mind putting your hat back on again?"

13. *Colley Cibber, Playwright*

Mr. Booth has discarded the version of *Richard III* as prepared for him by William Winter, and acted by him for some twelve years past, and restored to his repertory the well-known Colley Cibber version of Shakespeare's tragedy. To be sure there is some clap-trap, a goodly portion of Shakespeare, and a lot of Colley Cibber—but the mixture gives Mr. Booth a character which easily ranks with his Iago and Pescara in the scheming, subtle deviltry and sardonic humor with which Colley has padded it. (*Jan. 10th 1887*)

David Garrick, Colley Cibber and others took many liberties with Shakespeare's plays in making them fit the needs and conditions of their time. Garrick, of course, brought forth scenes that emphasized his own acting ability. Thus in *Richard III,* he opened the play with the funeral cortege.

When I was a youngster there was a famous English actor in this country who gave the best performance of *Richard III* we had seen. In those days it was not customary for a star to travel with a company. Towns such as Utica, Rochester, Buffalo, all had stock companies of their own. Stock actors were engaged for the season because they were "up" in all the parts of the standard drama so that when a famous actor like Forrest, Booth or Charlotte Cushman was announced, the actors could readily cast themselves for their parts in the plays. On this occasion the English actor sent his stage-manager four or five days ahead to rehearse the company in the movement of the play, not the words, as each star had his own peculiar ideas about where he was to stand and act. On this occasion the stage-manager wanted a tall and authoritative-looking super to utter one line.

In the opening act, Lady Anne and the members of the court are burying her father. Richard comes on the stage and stops the funeral procession. At this time Richard is not King, he is the Duke of Gloucester.

The stage-manager instructed the super to step forth when Richard stops the procession and say: "Stand back, my Lord, and let the coffin pass."

"Can you say that?" he asked.

"Certainly," the super replied. Thereupon he was given the Chamberlain's costume for the scene.

All day long the super rehearsed, repeating his one prized line. Night came at last, his great moment. The cortege passed, Richard made his appearance. The super as the Lord Chamberlain stepped forth and cried: "Stand back, My Lord, and let the Parson cough."

14. *Bob Keeley*

Bob Keeley, an actor in the days of old Covent Garden used to entertain his friends with great hospitality. Among the tradespeople with whom he dealt was one Berry, a grocer and fruit-seller, who dunned him before the time promised for payment. Keeley sent him this message:

> "I say, here's a mul Berry,
> You have sent in your bill Berry,
> Before it is due Berry.
> Your father, the elder Berry,
> Would not have been such a goose Berry,
> But you needn't look black Berry,
> For I don't care a straw Berry!"

(*Jan. 10th 1887*)

15. *Ellen Terry*

Charles Reade wrote this about Ellen Terry in his scrap-book: "Ellen Terry, a young lady highly gifted with what Voltaire justly calls *le grand art de plaire*. She was a very promising actress, married young to Mr. Watt, the painter. Unfortunate differences ended in a separation, and, instead of returning to the stage, she wasted some years in the country. In 1873 I coaxed her back to play Philippa at the Queen's Theatre and she was afterward my leading actress in a provincial tour. She played Helen Rolleston very finely (*Foul Play*). In 1875 engaged to play Portia at the Prince of Wales' Theatre; and her performance is the principal histrionic attraction, the Shylock of Mr. Coghlan being considered somewhat slow and monotonous. Ellen Terry is an enigma. Her eyes are pale, her nose rather long, her mouth nothing particular. Complexion a delicate brick dust, her hair rather like tow. Yet somehow she is beautiful. Her expression kills any pretty face you see beside her. Her figure is lean and bony, her hand masculine whether in movement or repose. Grace pervades the hussy. In character impulsive, intelligent, weak, hysterical—in short, all that is abominable and charming in woman." (*Aug. 25th 1887*)

Ellen Terry played all her great Shakespearean rôles when she was over fifty years and which shows that in good acting years have nothing to do with age. It has often been said that when a woman can enact the passion of Juliet she is too old for the character, while when a woman is the age of Juliet, and looks her youth, she cannot understand her passion. So years have nothing to do with age. One of the greatest Juliets who played the part under my management, was Madame Modjeska who was over sixty years old when she enacted the rôle. But she was so appealing, so effective and so dramatic that nobody questioned the matter of age. This fact holds true of all great parts. It is also true of beauty, for the audience forgets personal appearance when actresses are properly equipped to enact the big rôles which they play. Beauty attracts the eye at first but it fails to hold interest if there is no dramatic ability in back of it.

Actresses do not have to be beautiful if they have attractive features and pleasant faces and if they have the feeling and the emotion of the parts they play, it is quite sufficient, but added to this appearance must be a dramatic sympathy and without that no woman can be successful. I was asked once by a lady what the most important requisite for a young woman to possess to succeed on the stage was and I said personality. The matter went no further but personality must also be equipped with dramatic temperament for with these two qualities, we forget all about physical attributes.

16. *Thomas Barry*

The story is told that the late Thomas Barry, manager of the old Tremont Theatre, Boston, and Colonel Greene, editor of The Boston Post, were always at swords' points with each other. The manager never would send the editor tickets for "first night" performances, but there was always a criticism in The Post next day all the same. Once Barry was giving opera in English to poor audiences, and on the morning after "The Barber of Seville" was given, Colonel Greene remarked in The Post that the Barber appeared before a house not large enough to pay for the lather. (*Jan. 24th 1887*)

17. *Charm*

Here is a paragraph, from a Boston paper, which will interest the sensible female readers of *The Theatre:* "What made Ellen Terry so willowy in figure and so free and graceful in movement? Her clothes were loose. What enabled Mary Eastlake to squirm about so effectively as Helle? Her clothes were loose. What made Bernhardt serpentine and fascinating, and enabled her to step like some enthralling beast of the forest that had never known the curb of civilization? Her clothes were loose." (*July 27th 1887*)

18. *Madame Patti*

Madame Patti, says the *Paris Figaro,* has a fan on which are the autographs of all the sovereigns of Europe. Here are some of them:

The Czar, "Nothing is so soothing as your singing."

The Emperor of Germany, "To the ever-singing nightingale."

Queen Christina, "To the Spanish woman from a Queen who is proud to have her for a subject."

Queen Victoria, "If King Lear is right in saying that a sweet voice is a precious gift in a woman, you are the richest of women."

The Emperor and Empress of Austria merely signed.

Mr. Thiers, at the time he was President of the Republic wrote, "Queen of song, I stretch forth my hand to thee." (*Oct. 11th 1887*)

19. *Edith Kingdon*

Edith Kingdon, who is now Mrs. George Gould, and who owns as much of the earth as she cares to, presumedly, obtained her position at Daly's by a clever stratagem. She was performing a small part in the Boston Theatre while Mr. Daly's company was playing an engagement at the Museum. Miss Kingdon wrote to Mr. Daly asking for an interview, but had no response. Finally she conceived the idea of sending two seats for the Boston Theatre, and a carriage, to Mr. Daly. He could not resist, and attended the performance. The next day he sent her a note stating that he would call and see her, if agreeable. Now what did this clever girl do? She was living in an ordinary boarding house, but she went straightway to one of the leading hotels, hired a splendid suite of rooms, put on a handsome gown, which she borrowed from Rachel Noah, I believe, and then told Mr. Daly to come on. He did; she conquered. She became one of the most attractive actresses ever seen on Mr. Daly's stage, and then George Gould fell in love with her. (*Nov. 7th 1887*)

Edith Kingdon made her first application for a job to me at the old Madison Square Theatre. We had very long runs at the time and it was impossible to use this charming young lady's services. She afterwards worked for Augustin Daly who had frequent changes of bill. Daly had a keen eye for beauty as is shown by his management of Maxine Elliott.

20. *Maurice Barrymore*

Maurice Barrymore being asked the other day how his young son was, replied: "He is in the best of health— and I am very proud of him. He is in fact the only thing I ever owned that the newspapers have not accused me of taking from the French." (*April 30th 1888*)

21. *Sir Henry Irving*

Henry Irving tells this story: A haberdasher in London had joined the Junior Garrick Club and become inoculated with the idea of going on the stage. So he sold out his shop, reserving an ample supply of underwear, and invested the proceeds to eke out his salary as an actor. In time, his grand dreams of surpassing Kean and Kemble having departed, he was a humble utility man at the Theatre Royal, Manchester. But his invested money gave him income enough to provide a Christmas Eve supper for his associates at the theatre. One of them hesitated to accept, because the weather was so cold and his clothing was so thin and worn. Before the supper, the ex-haberdasher pushed this poor fellow into a bed-room saying, "There's a little present for you in here!" It was a suit of warm woolen underclothing. Fancy this poor actor's feelings, when, comfortably clad, his body and his heart equally warm, he took his place at table!

"I can feel that grateful warmth yet," exclaimed Irving, "for I was that poor actor!" (*Nov. 16th 1889*)

22. *Droll Stories*

There have been a great many droll slips in the text heard on the stage. Mrs. Langtry says the funniest she ever heard was: "Let us seek some nosey cook."

Fred Leslie says he once said: "I will step outside to get a fresh of breath air!"

One of the actresses in *The Bookmaker* once said: "Men can mope; but we women can only remain at home and smoke."

Frederick Terry, instead of saying, "I would rather die than let her become the wife of a blackleg such as you," said: "I would rather die than let her become the blackleg of a wife such as you!"

[123]

Edmund Glover once said: "Romeo's dead—stabbed with a black wench's blue eyes."

In *Money*, one of the actors once said: "Waiter, the buffsnox." Another impersonating Crabtree in *The School for Scandal*, talked about "a thullet in the borax." (*Feb. 1st 1890*)

23. *Lillian Russell*

Lillian Russell is indignant that a lot of people should think that, because a woman sings in comic opera, her private life is a whirlwind of doubtful propriety. She says: "The world, or at least that part of it which is interested enough in me to think at all, seems to think that my life is one round of joy and wild gaiety, full of diamonds and champagne and supper parties. Why, it is on the contrary, extremely monotonous and more quiet than that of most women who look after their own houses and go to the theatre once a week." (*Mar. 29 1890*)

Lillian Russell's real name was Helen Louise Leonard. She was born in Canton, Iowa, and educated at the *Convent of the Sacred Heart* in Chicago. While in the convent the sisters thought her so beautiful they wanted her to sit for a picture of St. Cecilia.

Lillian Russell was a woman of fine character and a fine poker player. I sent her out once in a play when the Lillian Russell Cigar was very popular.

"If this play draws as well as this cigar," I told her, "we'll all make money."

She was very generous and helped me a great deal in connection with my Actor's Fund Activities. In fact, one night in Pittsburgh when I was trying the town out for a benefit, she gave up a week's salary and a job in vaudeville just to help me out. She was joined in her efforts by a woman of wealth who lived there at the time. Her name was Fay Templeton.

9

SIR ARTHUR WING PINERO

ONE HAS but to contemplate the character, variety, literary and dramatic distinction of the works of Arthur Wing Pinero, to understand why he occupied such an exalted position in the dramatic world of his time. From the pathetic charm and wholesome beauty of *Sweet Lavender* and the whimsical and brilliant comedies of *The Amazons, The Schoolmistress, Dandy Dick, Trelawney of the Wells,* to the profound and impressive studies of character in *Iris, Quex, Ebbsmith, The Profligate* and the towering, tragic Hellenic qualities of *The Second Mrs. Tanqueray,* we have a revelation of mastery and resource, dramatic and intellectual, that reflects the tragic power and the satiric humor of the Greek dramatists. Profound, startling, caustic, remorseless in their development of character, the serious tales are unconventional and relentless epitomes of modern life. The author holds himself bound by no impulse to write for the crowd.

"I like to please the people with my work," Pinero once said, "for I take great pains and feel deeply on the subjects about which I write; but I must write in accordance with my convictions."

I had the honor of Pinero's acquaintance from 1887 until his death in 1934. I produced my first Pinero play

Sweet Lavender, at the old Lyceum on Fourth Avenue
on November 13th, 1888, with a cast that included W. J.
LeMoyne, Mr. and Mrs. Walcot, Mrs. Whiffen, Georgia
Cayvan, Herbert Kelcey, Henry Miller and Louise Dil-
lon. Later I produced many more of his plays in this
country. Few authors wrote plays that were more liked
by actors, not only because of the excellent parts, for
even the lesser ones gave the actors creditable opportunities, but because it was a delight for them to study
the well-written and fluent dramatic text, which made
memorizing easy.

During the period of my acquaintance with Mr.
Pinero, our relations, both personal and professional,
were always of the most delightful character. No man,
judging him by his serious works, was more unlike what
a student of the drama would conjure him to be. He
was gentle, amiable, the soul of good humor, with a
hearty, cordial manner, and a wealth of enthusiasm. He
had very black eyes and eyebrows, and a complexion so
ruddy, it seemed to reflect buoyant good health and a
love of outdoor sports. He was fond of his friends, and
was one of the most constant members of the famous
Garrick Club.

Pinero began as an actor in Henry Irving's company
Subsequently he appeared with the Bancrofts. But he
gave up acting and decided upon writing as a career; and
like many of the authors in England, his early connection
with the theatre was helpful. He married an actress, herself an excellent artist, and a woman of tact, charm and

alert intelligence. She retired from the stage when she became the dramatist's wife.

I once asked Pinero to write me a play of a certain style, and to emphasize my predilection for the subject. I suggested a considerable preliminary payment, which my one-time experience with Sardou taught me might gain instant approval. Mr. Pinero pondered over the matter for a day or two, but at the appointed hour, said, "Your offer is generous, but I can't see my way to accepting it. I must write according to my own subjects and my own convictions. But I am at work now on a piece. As soon as it is done I will send you the play as usual. Produce it if you think your public will like it. If not, it doesn't matter."

The play turned out to be *The Second Mrs. Tanqueray*—his greatest work! I *did* feel timorous about producing it. I thought our public was not ready for a theme that indicated so radical a change in my policy of productions at the Lyceum, in spite of the fact that it was a great work. George Alexander for whom it was written in London, was equally diffident. I suggested to the author a tentative series of matinees. Curiously enough Alexander made a similar suggestion. But the play was ultimately put into the evening bill at the St. James Theatre with Mrs. Patrick Campbell as the star and I produced it in America with the Kendals. It was much criticized here, but eventually it became recognized as a masterpiece.

But with all Mr. Pinero's works for the American

SIR ARTHUR WING PINERO

MRS. LANGTRY AS PAULINE

market, he was always modest in his ideas as to their possible financial value. The plays were written, and when completed, they were at the manager's call if he deemed them acceptable to the American public.

"Produce them," he said, "if you think the public wants them and that you are not likely to be out of pocket!"

Great men are usually modest. Each year the plays were sent. They were produced, and in most cases Mr. Pinero found his American clientage no less ardent and appreciative than his English patrons. In fact in the case of some of his comedies they succeeded even better than in England.

Several English authors were once wont to express their indifference to American acceptance of their plays, especially when appreciation failed to materialize. "We write," they said, "to please our own countrymen." Not so Pinero. He was as solicitous of the good will and favor of our public as his own; but he would not pander to the taste of either. He wrote from a strong sympathetic impulse; spending much time on his work; and like an artist, he was anxious that his work should be approved.

For that reason, he usually exercised a strict watch over the casting of his plays in London and America. He was not fond of subsequent changes or alterations. His plays evolved slowly and were written carefully. He lived in, and sympathized with every character. Every personage was completely drawn. The stage "business" was minutely indicated with the most scrupulous exactitude; so that in the hands of a sympathetic producer, the author's ideas were readily interpreted to the performers. In his later plays, as for instance, *His House in Order,* he sent his own ambassador from England to carefully impart his ideas to the local company. His works were usually so logically developed that subsequent revisions were not approved or indulged in.

In only one instance was any radical change ever made. That was in the ending and final scene of *The Profligate.* Conventional requirements favor happy endings. There is no need to insist upon needless pain and gloom. Plays do not suffer by the absence of sadness at the final curtain. But in his play, *The Profligate,* yielding to what repeated performances convinced him was the demand, Mr. Pinero changed the original tragic close of the play to one that brought a suggestion of future, if not immediate, happiness for the married couple. The author, however, acknowledged that this change admitted of no sacrifice on his part.

"I could," he wrote, "never allow the consideration of mere expediency to influence me in dealing with subjects upon which I feel deeply and write with all the earnestness of which I am capable. But as the sparing of Renshaw's life has in no way distorted my original scheme, as it affected the other actors in the play, the softening of the wife towards her husband now as it did originally, arises through the good offices of Murray."

This alteration which did not jeopardize the ethical effect of the situation, met with general approval.

The question of the place which Pinero holds among English dramatists of the last few centuries will always be a debatable one. Some scholars declare that *The Second Mrs. Tanqueray* was the best play since *The School for Scandal*. Whether this is true or not, I cannot say but there was one thing that Pinero and Sheridan held in common. They both understood humanity, the foibles of human nature.

John Hare, an English actor, once declared at a dinner at *The Cecil* in London, "Better a wine-glass of Pinero than a tumbler full of Ibsen." An author who sat nearby, commented, "Pour a wine-glass of Ibsen into a tumbler and fill it up with water and you have Pinero."

Both remarks, though clever, were untrue. Ibsen and Pinero were great enough to be taken without adulteration. And if I was more interested in the plays of Pinero it was because he wrote for a wider audience. As I have said before, the Ibsen cult is limited to the few who understand and appreciate his methods of construction and excellent workmanship.

10

THIS AND THAT

1. *What a Play Should Be To Succeed*

THE DEGREE of success attained by any play is based upon just how strong and deep are its elements of human interest. Most plays are necessarily works which might be safely classed as having a fair degree of general interest—but that is all. It is not enough that a story is properly and scientifically told. How often do authors despair at the failure of managers to appreciate their efforts, because their works are undeniably well-written, are properly constructed, have a certain degree of dramatic suspense, and in many respects meet with the technical requirements of the stage. Works of this kind, when produced, are applauded, fairly well praised by the critics, and, in a brief period of time, are withdrawn. The reason is that the play, while otherwise perfect as a technical work, does not stir the depths of human emotion deeply enough to arouse more than passing comment and indifferent interest.

This is the class of play that comes in shoals to the attention of producers; and these are frequently sifted by them, or their assistants, in order to find that work which may reveal a new writer of power, inspiration and charm, for the play that is a revelation of electric emotional strength, that is capable of thrilling the audience throug and through, or the comedy that is so striking in novelty, so fresh in invention, that it at once captivates the fancy, and stimulates the audience into roars of appreciation, is what is constantly sought.

All plays, however, need not possess these exalted qualities. They are seldom found, and works of simpler and more conventional quality abound, which, also, possess certain elements of success.

Among all the plays which experts can class as among desirable material, the most acceptable ones are those which make the strongest appeal to the emotions, and these works are based upon a fabric of heart interest. This is a topic of universal concern. A theme involving a sound love story is the first requisite and a safe one. I should, therefore, say the first requirement of a play is a love story. It may be romantic love, modern or mediæval love—any age, because the theme is of universal interest; but, as a matter of preference and safety, the subject from a modern view, is more readily marketable, and one which is more liable to appreciation and acceptance at the hands of the producer.

The story need not be new—there are few new subjects; but its complications and treatment should be fresh. The love story should be clear and distinct in the mind of the dramatist. The A B C of construction is to develop an obstacle in its course. This obstacle, reasonably, convincingly, and ingeniously created, must be removed. The subject may involve wealth, blood, caste, ambition—all of them can be treated in this environment. When these are affected by American conditions, it places the story in a more congenial environment for our audiences. One need not go far from our own life to find subjects which involve an expression of exalted virtue, nobility of purpose, supreme self-sacrifice, or renunciation, in contrast with the elements of greed, avarice, ambition, money-power, social distinction, and the other factors that make up the life of today. The life of the modern man and woman teems with conditions which are intensely dramatic. Selfishness is the keynote of mankind. Love is the sublimation of selfishness. All the world loves a lover, yet there is a greater and loftier theme than the human affections, and that is the problem which concerns human self-sacrifice and renunciation—a topic which surpasses all other subjects in absorbing interest when treated with skill and imagination. This theme, the love story, should be the dominating factor in the play; and all other elements should radiate from it; and the effort of the author should be centered upon the development of the subject which grows out of this theme, and not to be misled, diffusively, into other channels.

French and German audiences deprecate action at the expense of reflection. They prefer food for thought. So do American audiences; but American audiences think quickly, and are stirred more effectively when plays are treated with vivacity, and rapid sequences, and action, and necessarily, a convincing theme. There is much that is beautiful and real in our modern life that would furnish good, sound, interesting material for a successful American play.

2. *Fresh Eggs*

Some years ago in London when Dion Boucicault and E. A. Sothern were walking down the Strand one day, they paused before a pawn-broker's shop. It was very tawdry as they usually are, with a lot of old and musty articles exhibited in the window but in the center was a sign, easily read, "Fresh Eggs, For Sale."

The notice amused both of them very much and they went inside and got the shopkeeper to give them information about various things that he was offering for sale. For instance, an old painting.

"Why," said Mr. Sothern, "that's a storm at sea, isn't it?"

"No," replied the shopkeeper, "that's a scene of the western desert in the United States."

"Oh," said Mr. Sothern, turning to some other article, "this is interesting."

The shopkeeper was elated. From their curiosity he was sure that they were going to make some worthwhile purchase.

But finally Mr. Sothern said, "Well I don't think we'll take any of these, but we will take three fresh eggs."

3. *Critics*

The best-acted plays are not always seen by the critics, unless they attend more than once. Judgments of first night performances are the worst for actor and for au-

[135]

thor, so far as the purpose of good and effective criticism is concerned, for it is then, in the presence of the first audience, that the actor encounters the impression that his part makes, and it is from that performance that he is largely enabled to grasp its true proportions. Until he receives his impression from the audience, his part, so far as his acting is concerned, is a mere sketch, and until the author has received the same all-important and inspiring experience wrought from the consciousness of so many attentive, sympathetic souls, who are moved where he least expects it, and who remain dumb where he hoped for enthusiastic approval, and has touched and retouched the play again, it cannot be said to have received proper judgment from the critics. Thus on first nights the critic comes with his critical faculties severely attuned, while those on whom he exercises his functions are at their worst. The first night should be treated from the reporter's standpoint. Criticism should be delayed until after three or four performances.

4. *Jefferson on Shakespeare*

Joseph Jefferson who's fame became so enmeshed in the part of Rip Van Winkle that it was hard to tell whether it was Joseph Jefferson playing Rip Van Winkle or Rip Van Winkle playing Joseph Jefferson, was a great character actor. He played other parts besides Rip, notably that of Bob Acres in *The Rivals*. He was a natural born comedian but he was also good in pathetic parts as most comedians usually are. A notable instance is the

acting of Charlie Chaplin. Jefferson was a great Shakespearean scholar for he was ambitious to win renown as
Hamlet and Othello.

At one time when it was the vogue to argue over the
authenticity of authorship of the Shakespeare plays, many
claiming that Lord Francis Bacon really was the author,
a claim that had less substance than a bubble, I asked
Jefferson to preside at a literary dinner I was helping to
sponsor. He did so. During the course of his speech he
read the following lines which he had written for the
occasion:

"The question is this, if I'm not mistaken:
'Did Shakespeare or did Francis Bacon,
Inspired by genius and by learning too,
Compose the wondrous works we have in view.'

The scholar, Bacon, was a man of knowledge,
But inspiration isn't taught in college.
The wondering world asks, 'What is his profession?'

'He must have been a lawyer,' says the lawyer;
'He surely was a sawyer,' says the sawyer;
The druggist says, 'Of course he was a chemist';
The skilled mechanic dubs him a machinist.

The thoughtful sage declares him but a thinker,
And every tin-man swears he was a tinker.
And so he's claimed by every trade a factor;
Pardon, gentlemen, he was an *actor!*

[137]

I could fill up a lot of other stuff,
But I have taxed your patience quite enough.
In turning o'er the matter in my mind,
This is the plain solution that I find:

It surely is—'Who'er the cap may fit'—
Conceded that these wondrous plays, were writ.
So, if my Shakespeare's not the same,
It must have been another by that name."

5. *Edwin Booth Regrets*

The following is a letter written by Edwin Booth to a young man who wished to go on the stage. It is dated Boothden, Newport, July 27th, 1884. The letter is now the property of L. Stoddard Taylor of Washington, D. C., by whose kind permission I am permitted to quote it here.

"My dear Mr. de Zayas: I was indeed 'startled,' and I must confess, pained by your letter announcing your determination to abandon your profession for that of the stage, and in sincere frankness I beg you to reconsider the matter, for I really have no hope for a satisfactory result from such a change.

"The feelings which prompt you to take this step—I mean your 'love, enthusiasm and natural inclination,'—do *not* imply an ability for the art. There are hundreds of disappointed lives wasting on the stage where they felt—as you do—that a brilliant destiny awaited them.

"You may be able to recite in private with perfect

[138]

ease and propriety, even with excellence, and yet have no other qualification for the highest form of dramatic expression. It is a life of wearisome drudgery; and requires years of toil, and bitter disappointment, to achieve a position worth having.

"Mr. Field, of Boston, is to be my manager next season and I have already applied to him for positions in his already over-crowded company; but in vain. I have just sealed a letter to a young and talented lady friend in Paris containing Mr. Field's reply to my appeal on her behalf—the second letter of regret that he has sent me in response to favors I have asked for friends, consequently I will return the application you enclosed to me, for I know it is useless to send it to him. He has one of the few regular companies, engaged permanently—I mean in this country, and he keeps the best of them 'year in, year out,' as long as he can.

"You can form no idea of the many who solicit my influence—every season; professionals and amateurs; friends and strangers, of all qualities, male and female. It is very seldom that I can serve them, for managers prefer to judge for themselves, and as my 'support,' no matter how capable it may be, has been abused by the press for many years past, and will always be 'til the end of my career, my recommendation is not regarded by managers whose judgments are greatly influenced by what the critics say.

"I have known many who, like you, gave up home, friends and respected positions for the glitter of the

actor's callings and who now are fixed for life in subordinate positions, unworthy their breeding, education
and natural refinement. I beg you, as your friend and
sincere well-wisher, to abandon the mistaken resolve,
and enjoy the drama as a spectator, which pleasure, as
an actor, you would never know, and retain family,
friends and happy home that now are yours. Had nature
fitted me for any other calling I should never have
chosen the stage; were I able to employ my thoughts
and labor in any other field I would gladly turn my back
on the theatre forever. An art whose professors and followers should be of the very highest culture, is the mere
make-shift of every speculator and bore that can hire
a theatre or get hold of some sensational rubbish to cull
the public. I am not very much in love with my calling
as it now is (and, I fear, will ever be), therefore you see
how loth I am to encourage anyone to adopt it.

"I think you will take my advice as it is meant—in
sincere friendship and believe that my only wish is to
spare you sorrow that must follow the course you would
pursue. With cordial regards for yourself and family, I
am truly yours, Edwin Booth."

6. *Stagecraft*

The degeneracy of the stage has been a subject of
woe since the days of Shakespeare. I daresay that is why
the drama is so great a subject. That is why when a
really sound sensible play makes its appearance, it is
hailed with delight by press agent and public. But I am

not one of the numerous advocates who look for the purely educational quality in plays. A play, to prove popular—and by popular I mean liked and patronized by the multitude—must be sound drama and drama of the most convincing kind. By drama, I mean a transcript of life, either in its best form as it exists; or in its ideal form, as life ought to be, and thus embodying a wholesome story that is exalting in quality and uplifting in its effect. By its appeal to the imagination and the emotions, an element of ethical value is revealed that may or may not carry an educational quality; but if presented purely as an appeal to the intellect, it is doomed to failure—not the failure of impotent endeavor, of faulty construction, but the failure to command the attention of the large public, which should be the aim of the theatre. Yet such a play can enforce unobtrusively a lesson taught by a mimic experience that can be salutary and effective.

It is the multitude that makes a stage work valuable. The intelligence of the crowd is not as keen as the discrimination of the individual, for the crowd is more easily swayed by the display of feeling, passion and emotion, and so becomes more demonstrative. Literature as an evidence and revelation of good writing, is not to be barred; but the spoken language must be language that can be acted, that is the outgrowth and expression of the moods and qualities of the stage personages.

The drama today may not stand on an exalted plane, but its character is less concerned with so-called fine writing or intellectual effort than were the plays of the

[141]

early 18th century, when the art of acting had graver
significance than that concerned in the story-telling plays
of today. Then, literature of all kinds was not so readily
accessible to all classes as it is now, and the actors were
depended upon to spout with vehement effect, for it was
at the theatre that the public obtained more frequently
its acquaintance with the efforts of many great writers.

The character of the modern theatre has gradually
changed all this. The stage of the present does not pro-
trude itself into the auditorium, as it did in the early
days, but has been withdrawn within the proscenium to
make way for "picture" plays, rather than "platform"
or rhetorical exhibitions; and the declamation of the
actor has given way to the ensemble development of the
story.

The modern methods of lighting enable the auditor
to observe with exceeding clearness the faces of the actors; and so the illuminative "soliloquy" has been done
away with as being a form of bad art and lame construction. The skill of the author is united with the art of the
actor, to represent more convincingly the illusion which
a good play should create. In this way the stage reveals
now more lucidly the scope of the drama and is devoted
less to the display of spoken dialogue or verse.

The aim of a play and its purpose should be to show a
struggle of the mind, of will, of character, or event,
which include the picturing of the emotions and feeling
in a state of conflict.

What the stage gives us should be graphic. It should

depict society in its various phases; it should be devoted to the study of the manifestations of life revealed by its different classes that people the upper and lower stratum of humanity, and concern itself with the keen and searching problems of our own life.

Its appeal should come swift as a vivid human document transcribed with a keen dramatic hand, from life, not offered as a polemical treatise. For the latter, there is a public, but it is a limited one, and is the monopoly of students and scholars. Not Byron, Swinburne, Tennyson or Browning with their great faculties, could view life in the way to conform to the objective point of the real playwright. They are for the study, not the stage. Yet one would not deny them the dramatic form in which to convey their conceptions. Visualizing their characters on the stage of a theatre before an alert, listening audience requires the medium of another art. But the dramatic instinct in mankind is fostered by the drama of action and of character and of incident contributing to this action.

7. *Divorçons*

Victorien Sardou, the great French dramatist, always began his plays with a strong, vital, dramatic idea. His play, *Divorçons,* a signal success all over the world was based upon conditions then prevailing in France because of the absence of a divorce law.

It seems that young women when they were being wooed by young men always were obliged to have a chaperon present. No young woman of any reputation could see a man alone unless she was married to him. Many young girls married men of means, merely that they might be able to entertain other men whom they loved. A man would marry a girl sometimes out of affection, but more frequently for the money involved in the marriage arrangements. Then he would have an affair with some sweetheart away from the sanctity of the marital hearth. Therefore, when France passed a divorce law, the married women of France were delighted. They felt then that they could divorce their husbands and marry the men who had been wooing them despite wedlock, and so, of course, were eager for this change. But the crafty Sardou, in his play, *Divorçons,* uttered a word of warning. He virtually said, "Look out, you women of France! You think you may be disposing of a husband in favor of a lover. Stop and think whether you are doing a wise thing. Try and find out whether your husband is not the better man of the two." This was the idea that Sardou worked into his comedy. He brought the husband forward, who, perceiving the kind of a man that his wife was in love with, encouraged the young man to visit his home. His wife thereafter saw so much of him that she grew tired of his company. Before it was too late, she realized her error, sent him about his business and returned to the arms of her husband. This was the plot of the play. It was a warning to the women of France, and in spite of the fact that it was entertaining comedy, it had a very powerful sociological effect upon the matrimonial life of the country.

[144]

SARAH BERNHARDT AS MRS. CLARKSON

ELLEN TERRY AS PORTIA

8. *Book Ends*

Are you thinking of starting a library? If so perhaps a few suggestions of what every clever person should read would not be inapropos. Many collectors buy books merely because they are bound in Morocco or royal vellum. This is a fallacy.

"There is a kind of physiognomy," says Butler, "in the titles of books no less than in the faces of men, by which a skilled observer will as well know what to expect from the one as the other."

Jovial indeed must be the book published in 1644 with the following title, *A New Invention, or a Paire of Cristall Spectacles By Helpe Whereof May be Read so Small a Print, that What Twenty Sheets of Paper will Hardly Containe Shall be Discovered in One.*

Try to get that at your circulating library. It is not a discourse on the art of the optician, however, but a treatise on civil warfare.

Another neat and extremely rare old book by John Peters is entitled, *A New Way to Make Latin Verses whereby Anyone of Ordinary Capacity that only Knows the A, B, C, and can Count Nine, though he Understand Not One Word of Latin, or What a verse Means, may be Plainly Taught to Make Thousands of Hexameter and Pentameter Verses Which Shall be True Latin, True Verse and Good Sense.* Publication date was 679.

Perhaps you may not want to write Latin verses and

would be more interested in a book called, *Gentlemen, Look About You* which contains this motto on the title page:

> *Read this over if you're wise,*
> *If you're not, then read it twise;*
> *If a fool, and in the gall*
> *Of bitterness, read not at all.*

In 1559 appeared a book, entitled, *The Key to Unknown Knowledge, or a Shop of Five Windows*

> *Which if you do open,*
> *To cheapen and copen,*
> *You will be unwilling,*
> *For many a shilling*
> *To part with the profit*
> *That you shall have of it.*

A pamphlet published in 1703 had the following strange title: *The Deformities of Sin Cured, a Sermon Preached at St. Michael's, Crooked Lane, before the Prince of Orange, by the Rev. J. Crookshanks. Sold by Mathew Denton, at the Crooked Billet, Near Cripplegate and by all Booksellers.* The words of the text were *Every crooked path shall be made straight.* The Prince before whom it was delivered was personally deformed

In 1661 the old naturalist Lovell published a book at Oxford entitled, *Panzoologicomineralogia.* But this was nearly topped by Rabelais who proposed writing a book called, *Antipericalametaparhegedamphucribrationes.*

On the other hand, long before Elinor Glyn or Clara Bow were ever heard of, that is to say in about 1843, a work was issued with the laconic title of "*It.*" For days previous to its publication, advertising writers who would have been sensations on present-day radio broadcasts, placarded the walls of London with advertisements reading, *Buy IT. Order IT. Read IT*, etc.

Among other literary curiosities is a poem by Joshua Barnes, designed to prove that the authorship of *The Iliad* could be traced to King Solomon. This was, however no more absurd than the claim of the French critic, Daurat, in the 16th Century who pretended that he had found all of the Bible in Homer.

But the Golden Palm for title pages must go to a book by Gascoigne which reads, *A hundred sundrie flowres bounde up in one small poesie; gathered partly by translation in the fyne and outlandish gardens of Euripides, Ovid, Petrarch, Ariosto and others; and partly by invention out of our own fruitefull orchardes in England: yielding sundrie and divers swete savours of tragical, comical and moral discourses, both pleasant and profitable to the well-smelling noses of learned readers.*

9. *Salesmanship*

One of the most important things in the world is salesmanship. We are all salesmen whether we want to be or not. Whether you are a President, a King, an Actor, an Author or an Engineer, success or failure depends on how good a salesman you are. A King has to sell himself to his people. An actor has to sell himself to his audience. The canvas of an artist or the book of an author is nothing more nor less than one of his catalogues. Therefore I make no excuse for devoting a few pages to this important topic.

In any shop the most successful clerks are those who understand the art of salesmanship, for it really is an art, an art that has a certain psychological quality.

Once I went into a haberdashery on Broadway and asked a clerk if he had a certain article.

"No," he said abruptly, and turning from me, walked away.

I begged his pardon for troubling him and assured him I would never bother him again.

I went into another shop, but there the man said, "No, we don't have that article but you can get it at 838. They have quite an assortment there."

"Thank you," I said, "but maybe there is something more I want around here." And I looked over the display.

This showed the difference between the two characters. I daresay the last man will eventually have a shop of his own.

I said to a young saleslady in a department store one day, "If a woman stops at your counter and asks for some article of goods that you haven't got in stock, do not turn from her, but try and arouse her interest. For instance, say, 'That is a pretty gown you have on and of a charming design. We have a similar cloth here bu

I don't think it is as good as yours.' The chances are, due to this direct appeal to her vanity, she would at once be interested, and if she does not buy some other thing that day, she will certainly come to your place another day."

I put this sentiment in operation once myself, not through any principle, but a feeling of common sense. Common sense, you know, is a great factor in all professions. It is the oil that lubricates the wheels of industry. I was on the fourth floor of a big department store, purchasing a variety of toys for children, and while I was waiting to have them done up in packages, I saw a pretty young girl standing by a lot of mechanical toys.

I said to her, "Do you work here regularly, Miss?"

"No," she replied, "only during the holidays."

"What do you do?" I asked.

"I sell these toys."

"Are you selling any?"

"Nobody seems to want them," she sighed.

"No wonder," I told her. "You are so quiet everybody passes you. Why don't you make a little racket? Get the mechanical toys to moving. Let the bells ring and the horses run around and you will soon be surrounded by a group of inquisitive people anxious to know the cause of the commotion. Let me see if I can help you."

I started off, and a crowd of women gathered round me. And more important still, I commenced making sales rapidly, because I explained these were the most wonderful toys ever invented for children. By and by there were only two left.

"I will take one," a smiling lady said.

"Madam," I declared, "you ought to take both for they are most remarkable toys."

"But you see, Mr. Frohman," said she, "I have only one child."

Somehow or other she had recognized me as she watched my activities. Doubtless she was wondering how I had succeeded in progressing from the management of Salvini and Modjeska to "Mechanical Sam" in one generation.

There was a time when I was in Panama City with a touring party. After the chauffeur had shown us the sights of the town, I asked him where I could buy a cheap panama hat. He told me to go to Mrs. Thompson's where everything in the shop had its price marked on it. I asked him to let me off there.

When the car stopped in front of the shop, a man and two women, having heard the conversation, got out also. As my purchase was to be of modest character, I held back and allowed Mrs. Thompson to wait upon the other people first.

While I had my hat off, looking around at the goods, three ladies came in and asked the price of various things. They thought I belonged there because I had my hat off. I accepted the situation and sold them a number of articles. Then a lady pointed to one article and said, "That is rather pretty. What is the price of it?"

I looked and said, "$1.50."

"I think I will take it," she declared.

Then I discovered I had made a mistake. I did not see the other cipher. The price was $15.00.

I told her this but she did not take it. However she did make a number of other purchases.

Other people came in and I continued my operations while the old lady, Mrs. Thompson, was wrapping up parcels for the man and two women who had come in with me.

When we were all through, I scolded her and said, "You should not have allowed your son and daughter to go away from the shop on a day like this."

I did not know whether or not she had a son and daughter but I took a chance.

"I did not think I would do any business today," she explained, "and so I let them go."

"You should look in the paper every day and see when steamers are arriving and then you could be prepared for customers. Here you are wasting time tying up parcels when you might be selling goods."

At Colon, that night, after dinner at the hotel, I joined a party of people in the drawing-room. As I was introduced, one lady said, "Mr. Frohman of New York? Why, you are the gentleman who sold us the goods today in Panama."

Then her husband came over and said, "Mr. Frohman, my wife came back this evening from her shopping and told me she had been waited upon by a gentleman who was very polite."

"I am honored," I said, smiling, "for even though I

[151]

had but a small part in today's drama, I must have played it conspicuously, otherwise she would not have remembered me."

10. *Nora Lea*

Nora Bayes, whose death a few years ago came as a shock to everyone, had three adopted children, two small boys and a little girl named Nora Lea. I was very fond of the children and I used to have them frequently to my studio for luncheon, after which I'd take them to the Junior Art Club which was made up of the children of members of the Theatre Assembly that met once a month at the Hotel Astor. Nora Lea was about six years old at the time. The Junior Art kids used to give variety performances at the end of the Assembly meeting which were attended by members of the club and their friends. I'd usually have four or five kids on my lap while I watched the performances. Afterward there was dancing. On the occasion of which I write, I asked Nora Lea if she would dance with me. In a most dignified way, she said, "Oh, no, Uncle Dan." I of course felt that my first duty was to my guest, Little Nora, but when she said, "No," I found another little girl to dance with me. When Nora saw how this little kid and I were enjoying ourselves, she rushed forward, and with tears in her voice, said, "Oh, Uncle Dan, won't you dance with me?" I immediately did so.

When the entertainment was over, I said to her, "Now, Nora, you and your brothers must go home with your governess, have your supper and go to bed."

"Oh, no, Uncle Dan," said the little girl, "I am going to your studio with you."

Then I said, "No, Nora, you must go home, get your supper and go to bed."

"Oh, no," repeated little Nora, "I'm going to your studio and stay all night with you."

"Stay all night?" said I, with some amusement. "You can't do that."

"Why not?" she asked.

"Because the police won't let you," I said.

She looked annoyed, as she asked, "Not even for one night?"

When I next saw Nora Bayes she wanted to know what I was doing with her daughter.

11

PROBLEMS OF A MANAGER

THE FIRST problem for a manager is the question will the play he is going to produce be a success. This is a very big and wide question and covers a great many points of interest—dramatic, literary and human.

The impression of the play on the individual is different from the impression that a play will make on the mass. The psychology of the individual, his attitude and feelings undergo a change, or at least they vary to some extent when he is merely one of many. As a concrete individual he is calm, deliberate, judicial. With the mob he is part of it. He becomes with it emotional and demonstrative. You know how we shout and sing with the crowd and yell, "Hurrah!" and "Tiger!" and roar and laugh when swayed by the emotion and magnetism of numbers. So often a play will get over with a bang when least expected; and often the best considered effects go for naught when the heartiest response is expected. Dion Boucicault once told me as an evidence of this uncertainty that when he wrote his famous play, *The Shaughraun,* he had, as he thought, constructed a situation which was to elicit a big round of applause. It was a scene in which the villain of the play was to take up a gun and shoot the lover; but the Irish hero, as played by Boucicault, had, when he heard the villain's threat, abstracted the bullet from the gun to defeat his purpose, and left the stage. At this juncture Boucicault thought there would be a round of applause; but it was not forthcoming. But later in the scene when the villain was defeated from his malign purpose and Boucicault stuck his head out in triumph from the upper window, then the applause came. Now the author knew that there was a round of applause due to that action, but it did not come in the place expected. There again his instinct, dramatically, was correct. That is one reason why managers frequently try a play out-of-town—to ascertain not only where the effects lie, but whether the situations and the climax meet with ready response; and to learn where the laughter and applause come—if at the right places, or at all;—and where things go wrong that were expected to go right. These technical matters are then easily adjusted, and this preliminary experience suggests readily the necessary remedies.

But, of course, the more important matter to study and learn at these preliminary trials is whether the logic of the drama, or the theme of the play, carry conviction; and this is a good thing to do in these days of expensive productions and high salaries, because, if a play slumps on its first night in New York City, it is a most difficult thing for it to recover from the disastrous impression of failure; for the failure, like the instant success of a play, spreads with lightning-like velocity in all directions.

When a play is produced, for managerial purposes, it is more important to please the audience than the critics.

[155]

A critic is analytical and judicious, and he may discover artistic flaws in the structure of the work; but the audience is quickly moved by scenes and situations that appeal to its imagination and emotions even though the dramatic logic may sometimes be at fault. A divided press leaves much room for favorable speculation as to the popular value of a play; but when the newspaper critics are unanimous in their condemnation, it means that even the public signify a similar disapproval. Many a play succeeds in spite of hostile criticism; for "like the toad ugly and venomous it yet may wear a precious jewel in its head"; and this redeeming quality in the play, as I have said, may be, not the play, nor the plot, but often the manner of its treatment—the character of certain effective and compelling situations, or the special quality of the acting that may win the audience. The audience may, therefore, often acclaim a work that discloses artistic, ethical or dramatic defects or may ignore a play, and the play may languish, that meets with the approval of critical censors. Hence the preliminary value of the out-of-town productions. These are purely matters of business interest, and, of course, have no part in the consideration of the Drama as an academic proposition; but then I have only been associated with the Drama in combination of the artistic with the business side.

With regard to the out-of-town experiences I might mention one or two episodes that indicate their value. One is the experience disclosed by the fate of the musical play entitled, *The Royal Vagabond*. It was a failure on its out-of-town preliminary canter. George M. Cohan was called in. He saw that the authors of the book had treated the subject with operatic seriousness; so he turned the story into a comedy and translated every dignified and serious situation into rampant and roguish farce, jazzing up the music and adding several numbers and many lines of his own. Thus he turned what had been up to that date an eighty thousand dollar loss, into a property that later brought considerable return to the owners.

Another case was that of the play produced by David Belasco at my theatre, entitled *Tiger Rose* with Lenore Ulric as the star. This was a simple little melodramatic tale of the West. On its trial tour, Belasco saw that the value of the story alone was too slight to hold the interest of a New York audience for two hours and a half; so he devised a series of skillful stage scenes and effects, not extraneous but helpful to the unfolding of the tale, such as the accompaniment of a real rainstorm, clever lighting effects, charming flashes of sunlight and the softening glow of moonlight through the woods and every possible quality that expert knowledge of stage technique could suggest. Thus the story became enhanced by the addition of these stage resources and became one of the most interesting theatrical entertainments of the season.

You may say that this is not the art of the Drama. No, but it belongs to the business of the theatre—that branch of the theatre which seeks to maintain itself by entertaining the public and at the same time paying expenses. But

[157]

there are plays of a higher quality than those I mention that are subject to the same and even more radical changes before they are submitted to the view of the public and which are turned from impending disasters into pre-eminent successes. An instance in my own experience of this class concerns the play entitled, *If I Were King,* which was played some years ago by Edward H. Sothern when he was under my management. Among the plays Mr. Sothern and I had purchased was this work by Justin McCarthy which he desired me to produce. I watched the two or three rehearsals and saw that its structure needed altering. It was a story about François Villon, the poet of ancient France, who for a joke was made the king's chamberlain and who had hoped to prove to the king that he was more than the street brawler. But I felt that the motive was not strong enough. Villon should prove it not to the king, but to a woman, and to a woman of high degree, who had spurned him when she first saw him, and so I suggested to the author to take the theme of *The Lady of Lyons* and rewrite the play on these lines. He did so and after a delay of four or five weeks the play was produced and was one of the greatest successes in Mr. Sothern's repertoire; and this success was due to the fact that the story in spite of its archaic quality and flamboyant character was based on the eternal and enduring subject of the love of man for woman, the clash of wills and the conflict of circumstance.

Shakespeare tells us that the actor is the abstract and

brief chronicle of his time. By this we derive the meaning that the plays in which the actor appears represent to the audience the spirit, the genius, the aspiration and the trend of their own time. It is a fact that we are inclined little these modern days to the old-fashioned, turgid, tragic dramas of the past. Occasionally, as acting *tour de force* for some star we might be interested for a brief time in a special display of histrionism. The tragic dramas of the Greek stage or those of the Elizabethan dramatists are not for modern audiences accustomed to their modern forms of life and methods of thought. Once upon a time when it was a popular function in England to revive the dusty dramas of the distant past, Charles Lamb said in a spirit of mockery, "Away with the modern drama! I will write for antiquity." As dramatic curiosities they are interesting and even educational and enlightening to students of the Drama, but they are not for popular consumption.

I have heard it frequently said that Shakespeare was meant to be *read,* not to be acted, and that the reading of Shakespeare revealed more of the poet's genius than did the acting of his characters. But the man who said this knew little of the art of the dramatist. The opportunities for acting and for revealing the distinct qualities of the artist who impersonates the big characters in the Shakespeare plays are simply limitless. The dramatist gives the artist opportunity; it depends upon the artist to avail himself of it. His success with an audience depends entirely upon his resources of expression, of imagination

[159]

and upon the quality of his dramatic temperament. Many an actor has revealed himself as a brilliant and capable performer, an impersonator of modern roles, but when he essays Shakespeare, Shakespeare finds him out.

In connection with what I said of the reading of Shakespeare as compared with the acting of the characters, let me give one or two instances to show the difference. Let us take the scene in *Macbeth* when Macbeth says to his wife: "Duncan comes tonight." She replies, "And when goes hence?" This would mean little in the reading. But when she receives this information she looks up quickly, approaches her lord with two or three footsteps, grasps him by the arm, and with sinister aspect whispers to him, "And when goes hence?" In this action, gesture and manner, Macbeth sees the crafty and sinister purpose of his wife. He starts back, glaring at her, and virtually saying to himself, "My God, she means murder!" But he only says, "Tomorrow, as he purposeth." Here is where the simple lines are illustrated by expressive and very illuminative action on the part of the actress.

There is another effect similar in the value of its illustration in Henry VIII. Katherine's enemy is Cardinal Wolsey. He and Cardinal Campeius sit together, dominating the accused Queen. Cardinal Campeius has just spoken to Katherine and has taken his seat beside Wolsey. Katherine's lines are simply, "My Lord Cardinal, to you I speak." Simply this and nothing more. But in the acting of these few words a tremendous and startling

MADAME RISTORI AS LADY MACBETH

BEN JONSON

effect is reached by the actress if she is big enough as was Siddons and our own Charlotte Cushman. In acting this scene, Katherine says, "My Lord Cardinal." Upon this Cardinal Campeius arises. Not referring to him, Katherine bows to him humbly, then straightens up with full majesty, revealing loathing and resentment, and with a big gesture, pointing toward Wolsey, in tones of thunder hurls the words, "To you I speak," with an effect that is startling.

Edmund Kean's first appearance in London on that memorable occasion as Shylock, which startled the entire English stage by the unexpected exhibition of the actor's brilliant genius, was one of the most remarkable in the entire history of the drama. He comes in, as you all know, with Gratiano, who had called upon him to borrow three thousand ducats for his friend, Antonio, whom Shylock loathes. So on entering, Shylock repeats Gratiano's request. He says in a tremendously significant and sinister way, "Three thousand ducats, and for three months—and Antonio bound." But the intense loathing, hatred and vindictiveness and the accompanying gesture, containing an indication of his resolution to comply with the request because it would place Antonio in Shylock's power, was so tremendous in its awesomeness and its suggestion of evil that the audience was startled, in fact transfixed, by the actor's appalling ferocity. The entire performance on that evening, as I have written elsewhere in this book, was undoubtedly one of the most memorable ever given on an English stage. Coleridge said that Kean's performance was like reading Shakespeare by flashes of lightning. When the actor came home that night to his wife, to her inquiry he said, "The pit rose at me," a line which has become memorable.

Simplicity of diction and effectiveness of the appeal to the minds of the audience are shown throughout Shakespeare's treatment of his speeches in their simple dramatic form. When Macbeth sees the ghost of Banco and says, "Avaunt! and quit my sight. Thy bones are marrowless; thy blood is cold! There is no speculation in those eyes which thou dost *glare* with," there is no difficulty in feeling his alarm or in understanding his words, and when Macbeth in his fear-wrought mind thinks he sees the dagger and says, "Is this a dagger which I see before me—its handle toward my hand? Come, let me clutch thee. I have thee not and yet I see thee still." Note the utter simplicity of these Anglo-Saxon words and yet the tremendous opportunity for the actor to show his talents. Because the words are so simple, they present greater opportunities for expression.

And Othello when he leaps upon Iago in that one brief moment of doubt, takes him by the throat and says, "If thou dost slander her and torture me never pray more! Horror on horror's head accumulates for nothing canst thou to damnation add deeper than this!" All these speeches are projected on the simplest Anglo-Saxon methods of speech. But when Shakespeare wished to surrender himself to scenes of description of places, conditions, or moods, he expressed himself through a form of poetry and a graciousness of diction that have made him the unparalleled poet as well as the supreme dramatist of all time.

The great asset of the actor is, therefore, his capacity for expressing earnestness with the eloquence of a vivid and flexible temperament so pervading and vibrating that it touches everyone in the audience. It is this quality of personality that makes one actor greater than another. It is said that when David Garrick and another great actor named Spranger Barry thrilled London each with his performance of Romeo, an actress of the time who had played with them both was asked which of the two Romeos appeared to her the most effective.

"Well," she said, "when Garrick plays Romeo I feel that I must come down from the balcony to him. When Barry enacts the rôle I feel that he is coming up to me."

Today, the prevailing taste for plays runs naturally toward subjects of modern interest. We are interested in the life and thought and aspirations around us. Subjects for drama are not always new but there are always new and contemporaneous angles of interest in all subjects that affect humanity. The old Greek dramatist, Terence, once said, "I am a man; therefore all things that interest man interest me." I daresay the modern dramatists would translate this in saying that being a man all that interests woman interests him, for the essential foundation of most plays is based on sex interest.

Many plays win favor that do not always embody the

[163]

conventional or traditional methods either as to subject or treatment. Some local interest may give special favor to certain works, like fashions in clothes. Patriotism and war may develop certain traits of character that find response for the time being, but the essential value of a play depends on its degree of human interest, that strikes at once into sympathetic contact with all classes—the gallery as well as the orchestra circle—the touch of nature that makes the whole world kin.

In all this the art of the dramatist will live, as the art of the painter and that of the sculptor endures; but the flame of the actor's genius goes out with his death, and the eloquence which he inspires and with which he transports the hearts and imagination of his hearers, dies with him, and he remains barely a memory. Macbeth discloses this thought in one of the most sublime speeches of Shakespeare at the end of that tragedy; the lines beginning: "Tomorrow—and tomorrow—and tomorrow creeps in this petty pace from day to day to the last syllable of recorded time," and ending with: "Life's but a walking shadow; a poor player who struts and frets his hour upon the stage and then is heard no more."

12

RAMBLES IN ANECDOTIA OVER MAIN-TRAVELED
ROADS

1. *Junius, the Epicurean*

JUNIUS BRUTUS BOOTH was at times the victim of strange
fancies. Once he decided to be an absolute vegetarian,
and while possessed of this idea he was traveling on a
Western steamboat, and happened to be placed at the
table opposite a solemn Quaker, who had been attracted
by the eloquent conversation of the great actor.

"Friend," said the Quaker, "shall I not help thee to
the breast of this chicken?"

"No, thank you," said Booth.

"Then shall I not cut thee a slice of this ham?"

"No, friend, not any."

"Then thee must take a bit of the mutton; thy plate
is empty," persisted the Quaker.

"Friend," said Booth, in deep, stentorian tones, "I
never eat any flesh but human flesh, and I prefer that
raw!"

The old Quaker was speechless and his seat was
changed to another table at the next meal.

2. *Henry Came Forth*

On another occasion the elder Booth was billed to
appear as King Henry IV at the Old Bowery Theatre

on a certain evening. A large and fashionable audience assembled, and at the proper time the curtain rose. As is well known the elder Booth occasionally took a drop too much, and it was seen from the maudlin way in which he stumbled through the first scene on this occasion that he must have been indulging rather copiously. At last a few hisses from the gallery caught his ear. He suddenly stopped and, advancing to the footlights, said, "Ladies and gentlemen, you see that I am not in good condition to play tonight. But if you will only wait five minutes while I go behind the scenes to cool my head in a pail of water, I'll come out and show you the damnedest King Henry you ever saw in your life!"

3. *Macklin and Johnson*

Charles Macklin was disputing with Dr. Johnson on a literary subject. To emphasize his point the latter quoted Greek.

"I do not understand Greek," said Macklin.

"A man who argues should understand every language," declared Johnson acidly.

"Very well," said Macklin, and gave him a quotation in Irish.

4. *Boucicault Again*

Dion Boucicault met H. J. Byron, the playwright and they fell to discussing the comparative good fortunes of their plays on the stage.

"I dread a first night," said Byron, "for one of my new plays. I am eternally haunted by the fear of failure."

"That is strange," said Boucicault. "I never fear anything. I am as confidant as possible, whatever my new play may be."

"Ah," said Byron, "your confidence is easily understood. You are, of course, never nervous about your pieces, because they have invariably been played before."

5. *Wilde*

Oscar Wilde arrived at his club one evening, after witnessing a first production of a play that was a complete failure.

A friend said, "Oscar, how did your play go tonight?"

"Oh," was the lofty response, "the play was a great success but the audience was a failure."

6. *Shaw*

And that reminds me, though I don't know why, of Bernard Shaw who was called out one evening by an enthusiastic audience to make a speech after his play had made a big hit. Of course he complied because everything he says is a speech, so he was not caught unprepared. As he was about to say a few hundred words, a man hissed from the gallery. Shaw took a step forward, pointed up toward the man and said, "You're quite right, sir, but what are you and I against so many?"

Frank Harris once said, "Shaw has no enemies and none of his friends like him." Which was a droll statement since the very comment was couched in Shaw's own language. It was a disciple speaking. Later Shaw wrote the introduction to the Wilde biography which Harris wrote, and still later Harris wrote the life story of Bernard Shaw. If these were enemies, the world would be a better place if it were peopled with more of them.

7. *Young Werther*

One day when William Makepeace Thackeray arrived at his club, some of his friends were discussing a novel written by the famous Johann Wolfgang Von Goethe, called, *The Sorrows of Young Werther*. They all claimed that the book was far too big for the slenderness of the story. Thackeray agreed with them, and he said, "Give me a few minutes' time and I will condense the story." So he retired for awhile, and came back later with these lines:

> "Werther had a love for Charlotte
>   Such as words could never utter;
> Would you know how first he met her?
>   She was cutting bread and butter.
>
> Charlotte was a married lady
>   And a moral man was Werther,
> And, for all the wealth of Indies,
>   Would do nothing for to hurt her.
>
> So he sighed and pined and ogled,
>   And his passion boiled and bubbled,
> Till he blew his silly brains out,
>   And no more was by it troubled.

    Charlotte, having seen his body
      Borne before her on a shutter,
    Like a well-conducted person,
      Went on cutting bread and butter."

8. *Renown*

The following paragraph appeared in a Dublin paper after the first appearance of Mrs. Siddons on that stage: "Last night Mrs. Siddons, about whom all the world has been talking, exposed her beautiful, adamantine, soft and lovely person for the first time, in the Theatre Royal, Smock-Alley, in the bewitching, melting, and all tearful character of Isabella. From the repeated panegyrics in the London newspapers, we were taught to expect the sight of an heavenly angel: but how were we supernaturally surprised into the most awful joy, on beholding an earthly goddess! The house was crowded with hundreds more than it could hold, with thousands of admiring spectators, that went away without a sight. This extraordinary phenomenon of tragi-excellence, this star of Melpomene, this comet of the stage, this sun of the firmament of the muses, this moon of blank verse, this Queen and Princess of tears, this Donellan of the poisoned bowl, this Empress Rusty-fusty of the pistol and dagger, this chaos of Shakespeare, this world of weeping clouds, this Juno of commanding aspect, this Terpsichore of the curtains and scenes, this Proserpine of fire and earthquake, this Katterfelto of wonders, exceeded expectations, went beyond belief, and soared above all

[169]

the powers of description. She was nature itself. In short, she was the most exquisite work of wit. Where expectations were raised so high, it was thought she would be injured by her appearance; but it was the audience who were injured. Several fainted even before the curtain drew up; but when she came to the scene of parting with her wedding ring, ah, what a sight was there! The very fiddlers in the orchestra blubbered like hungry children for their bread and butter! and when the bell rang for music between the acts, the tears ran in such plentiful streams from the bassoon player's eyes, that they choked the finger-stops, and making a spout of the instrument, poured such a torrent on the first fiddler's book, that, not seeing the overture was in two sharps, the leader of the band actually played it in one flat: but the sobs and sighs of the groaning audience and the noise of corks from the smelling bottles, prevented the mistakes between the flats and sharps being perceived. One hundred and nine ladies fainted, forty-six went into fits, ninety-five had strong hysterics. The world will scarce credit the assertion, when they are told, fourteen children, five old women, a one-handed sailor, and six common-councilmen, were actually drowned in the inundation of tears that flowed from the boxes and galleries, to increase the briny flood in the pit. The water was three feet deep; and the people that were obliged to stand upon the benches, were, in that situation, up to their ankles in tears."

9. *Garrick's Bible*

David Garrick, whenever he wished to insure secrecy, always solemnly pronounced, "Swear! will you swear? Will you take your oath?"

Upon the actor replying, "Yes, sir," Garrick would go to his bookcase, take out a volume of Shakespeare and present it to the performer, who would kiss it with utmost solemnity; that ceremony over, the mighty secret was imparted.

10. *His Dinner*

Garrick once gave a dinner at his lodgings to Henry Fielding, Macklin, Havard, Mrs. Cibber and a few others. Vails to servants being much the fashion at the time, Macklin and most of the company gave Garrick's man (David, a Welshman) a shilling or half a crown; while Fielding very formally slipped a piece of paper in his hand, with something folded on the inside. When the company were all gone, David seemed to be in high glee. Garrick asked him how much he had received.

"I can't tell you, Sir," said Davy, "till I've counted it. Here's half a crown from Mrs. Cibber, Got bless hur—here's a shilling from Mr. Macklin—here's two from Mr. Havard, and here's something more from the poet, Got bless his merry heart."

By this time David had unfolded the paper when, to his great astonishment he saw that it contained no more than one penny. Garrick felt nettled at this; and next day he spoke to Fielding about the impropriety of jesting with a servant.

"Jesting!" said Fielding with seeming surprise, "far from it; I meant to do the fellow a real service; for had I given him a shilling or a half crown, I knew you would have taken it away from him; but by giving him only a penny, he had a chance of calling it his own."

11. *And His House*

When Garrick showed Dr. Johnson his fine house, gardens, statues, pictures and other treasures at Hampton Court, instead of a flattering compliment, which was expected, the Doctor said, "Ah, David, David, David," clapping his hand on the little man's shoulder, "these are the things that make a death-bed terrible."

13

RICHARD BURBAGE

1

A PLAY that does not meet all the requirements that an audience expects needs very good scenery to help the effect, but a good story, a good play, a good drama, well-acted does not require scenery of pronounced quality. One of the poet-laureates of England, Austin Dobson, once wrote a poem that admirably illustrates this point. It was called *When Burbage Played* and read as follows:

"When Burbage played, the stage was bare
Of fount and temple, tower and stair,
Two broadswords eked a battle out;
Two supers made a rabble rout;
The Throne of Denmark was a chair!

And yet, no less the audience there
Thrilled through all changes of Despair,
Hope, Anger, Fear, Delight and Doubt,
    When Burbage played.

This is the Actor's gift; to share
All moods, all passions, nor to care
One whit for scene, so he without
Can lead men's minds the roundabout,
Stirred as of old these hearers were
    When Burbage played."

2

It is not odd that Burbage should have inspired Dobson for Richard Burbage had the faculty of stimulating the minds of poets including that of William Shakespeare. Burbage it was for whom most of the Shakespeare plays were written. He also was the first to act many of the plays of Ben Jonson, truly achievement enough for any man. Burbage's most celebrated part was that of Richard III and it is in reference to this that one of the best known stories of Burbage and Shakespeare has to do. It was related in old London how on a certain occasion Burbage had a rendezvous with a celebrated lady but when he arrived at her home he was told by one of her servants that the lady was occupied at that moment, rather pleasantly, with William Shakespeare. Burbage was very angry and fumed and fussed about and insisted that the servant go in and make known to his mistress the fact of his arrival. But in some manner, Shakespeare intercepted the message and sent out a terse answer to the effect that William the Conqueror came before Richard III.

I can imagine how angry Burbage was as he stalked away. Perhaps in his next performance he purposely fumbled his lines in order to vex Shakespeare. In those ancient days men hungered for knowledge. There were few books and only the wealthy had access to them. In England there were no good sculptors and few artists of distinction. Those wealthy enough to afford to have their

[174]

portraits painted used to send to the continent for artists to come to England on the commission. Most of them came from France. Life indeed must have been dull and there is little wonder that the masses clutched at any snatch of humor no matter how low and vulgar. It was the era in which legend and folklore were at their height of fashion, and stories were handed down preciously from one generation to another like jewels that must be carefully preserved.

The theatre was the one great source of amusement and greater still of education. For this reason Shakespeare, who was in favor with Queen Elizabeth, wrote *Richard II, Henry IV, V, VI, VIII,* and so forth, not as dramatizations, but to give vast crowds of people who could neither read nor write some idea of their former rulers. When he stopped to write a play for dramatic purposes, he wrote such plays as *Romeo and Juliet* and *Othello,* out of his feeling and sympathy for human nature. Shakespeare was somewhat of a politician. He knew how to keep in the good graces of Queen Elizabeth. For instance, when he introduced the genial character of Falstaff in one of his lesser plays, it so intrigued the Queen that he wrote *The Merry Wives of Windsor* especially for her, in which Falstaff had a leading part. Falstaff had a great many comic ups and downs in this play and Queen Elizabeth enjoyed it immensely. Ever since, it has been one of Shakespeare's most popular comedies.

Sometimes I wonder how far-reaching has been the educational power that Shakespeare wielded over England. He molded the minds of his audiences and undoubtedly in many instances he must have imbued them with a desire for better things. And, therefore, Shakespeare more than anyone else has shaped the character of England.

During this past theatrical season we have had one of the most amazing Shakespearean presentations on record, that of Maurice Evans in King Richard II. Never until this year has the play been produced with any semblance of success. Then Maurice Evans attempted it. How Shakespeare would have laughed if he could have known that Richard II would be a success finally, but not until more than three hundred years after his death.

I asked Maurice Evans how much it cost to produce Richard II and he told me that it was somewhere around $23,000.

I said, "That's probably more than Shakespeare paid for all his plays because he had no scenery."

For this reason, occasionally he appealed to the audience to use their imaginations in lieu of stage setting, as for instance in Henry V when he says, "You must work, work your thoughts."

3

Old writers speak of the year 1602 dying in gloom. The Queen was dying. Her successor was doubtful. There were rumors and realities of plague and Hamlet's spirit hovered over all, "O cursed spite, that ever I was born to set it right." Always in times of plague, the theatre was a place of peril, especially when popular

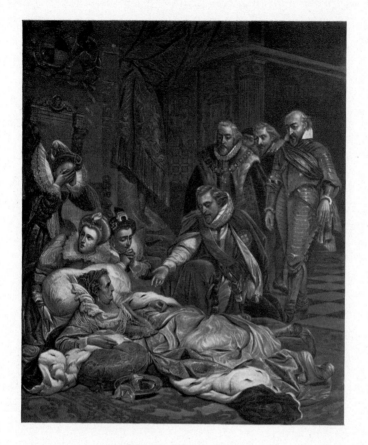

DEATH OF QUEEN ELIZABETH

RICHARD BURBAGE

actors were playing, due to the crowds that flocked to see them. At a later date we have a notable example of this in the life of David Garrick and what was popularly known as Garrick Fever. And again during the days of Mrs. Siddons when similar pestilence broke out. But in the time of Richard Burbage, greater care was taken as a safe-guard to health for I find an old warrant dated 8th February 1603-04 issued to Richard Burbage "for the maintenance and Relief of himself and the rest of his company being prohibited to present anie plaies publiquely in or near London, by reason of the great peril that might grow through the extraordinary concourse and assemblie of people to a newe increase in the plague till it shall please God to settle the cittie." The amount of the grant was £30.

For more than eighty years the name of Burbage was intimately connected with the drama in England. James Burbage, father of Richard was one of the owners of the famous Blackfriars Theatre which was built in 1576, following the issuance of a licence by the Queen on the 10th of May 1574. As a man, James Burbage was held in respect by everyone but his fame in no way equals that of Richard, his son, who built the Globe Theatre on the Bankside in the spring of 1594. The builder was Peter Streete who also undertook the erection of the Fortune Theatre in Golden Lane. The Globe had only two doors, one leading into the rear, the other into the body of the theatre where the audience was accommodated.

[177]

It is possible that the theatre was named the Globe because of the sign which it displayed but I prefer the suggestion that it was inspired by the words of Shakespeare: "All the world's a stage and all the men and women merely players."

On St. Peter's Day, June 29th 1613, the Globe was destroyed by fire and it speaks well for the management to record that even though the flames burst out without warning during a performance, all escaped by two small doors. Not a single life was lost nor a person injured. Henry Wotton, who was present at the play, wrote the following account of it three days later in a letter to his nephew: "Now to let matters of state sleep, I will entertain you at the present with what hath happened this week at the Bankside. The King's players had a new play, called *All is True,* representing some principal pieces of the reign of Henry the Eighth, which was set forth with many extraordinary circumstances of pomp and majesty, even to the matting of the stage; the knights of the order, with their Georges and Garter, the guards with their embroidered coats and the like: sufficient, in truth, within a while, to make greatness very familiar if not ridiculous. Now King Henry, making a mask at the Cardinal Wolsey's house, and certain cannons being shot off at his entry, some of the paper, or other stuff wherewith one of them was stopped, did light on the thatch, where, being thought at first but an idle smoke and their eyes more attentive to the show, it kindled inwardly, and ran round like a train, consuming, within less than an hour, the whole house to the very grounds. This was the fatal period of that virtuous fabric, wherein yet nothing did perish but wood and straw, and a few forsaken cloaks: only one man had his breeches set on fire, that would perhaps have broiled him, if he had not, by the benefit of a provident wit, put it out with bottle ale."

Ben Jonson was another interested spectator of the conflagration and confirms the report that the roof was of thatch. He further points out that there was a ditch surrounding the theatre filled with water so that the fire might easily have been extinguished had there been any means of applying it.

In the following spring the Globe was rebuilt and the King and court helped liberally with funds. That it was a superior building to the old one there can be no doubt since the roof was of tile, and it was large and far more ornamental but its construction was scarcely less inflammable since it was undoubtedly built of wood.

Thereafter the King's servants continued to perform there except on those occasional interruptions when the ghost of plague replaced the ghost of Hamlet's father and the theatre was closed for indeterminate periods. The last record of the Globe Theatre is 1647 after which it was pulled down.

4

Richard Burbage was perhaps Shakespeare's greatest character for in this one character, all other characters lay hidden, as though in the wings, to emerge when

[179]

called upon, to strut his part and then give way to other characters. In Shakespeare, Burbage received his greatest glory. Shakespeare died in 1616 but while Burbage still lived, few there were who realized that Shakespeare was dead. When Burbage died on March 13th 1619, then died Shakespeare, so truly had the two become identified with one another. Burbage inspired Shakespeare to greater effort. He was so versatile, there did not seem to be a part he could not read into life, and this great power was undoubtedly fed by the quality of the parts which his friend devised for him.

With Burbage dead, all London mourned. And Thomas Middleton wrote:

"Astronomers and Stargazers this year
Write but of four eclipses, five appear,
Death interposing Burbage and there staying
Hath made a veritable eclipse of playing."

While another of his contemporaries who preferred to remain anonymous wrote:

"What a wide world was in that little space,
Thyself a world, the Globe thy fittest place!
Thy stature small, but every thought and mood
Might thoroughly from thy face be understood.
And his whole action he could change with ease
From ancient Lear to youthful Pericles."

14

O RARE SIR WILLIAM D'AVENANT

1

IT WAS fitting that William D'Avenant should have been born the son of a wine-maker, for wine was prominent among his many loves throughout his life. He lived furiously, loved intensely, fought valiantly but withal he was a trifle careless for somehow, somewhere in his numerous adventures, he lost his nose and thereafter lived in constant dread that his eyes might fail for he had no proboscis upon which glasses might gracefully recline. But I am jumping ahead of my story, even as so frequently William D'Avenant jumped ahead of his.

John D'Avenant, his father, kept the Crown Inn, St. Martin's Orchard, Oxford, England. He was known as a vinter, a man of some opulence. In Oxford the business of vinter was exclusive, the privilege of granting licenses being vested in the University by a Charter of Henry VIII and later confirmed by an act of Parliament. John D'Avenant though he kept a famous Inn, had none of the jovial appearance of an Innkeeper. He was grave and melancholy. He never laughed. In the Oxford of his day even a smile would have been headline news or, in the absence of newspapers, a morsel for universal gossip. The family of D'Avenant is believed to have emanated from the Avenants of Lombardy.

William's mother was a woman of great beauty, whose conversation and wit attracted everyone, including William Shakespeare who always lodged at the Crown Inn on his annual journeys from London to Warwickshire. Long afterwards, William D'Avenant used to suggest to his drinking companions that Shakespeare might have been his father, in fact he hoped he was. Among the manuscripts left by a contemporary, Anthony Wood, is recorded the following: "Now Sir William would sometimes, when he was pleasant over a glasse of wine with his most intimate friends, including Sam Butler, author of *Hudibras,* say that it seemed to him that he writt with the very spirit that Shakespeare did, and seemed contented enough to be thought his son."

Personally, after going through many volumes in research, I cannot take this suggestion very seriously. Even Pope has left testimony tending to give the assertion credence for he wrote: "His father's house being frequented by the famous Shakespeare, his poetical genius, in his youth was by that means very much encouraged, and some will have it that the handsome landlady, as well as the good wine, invited the tragedian to those quarters."

Shakespeare was admired by all the family including the father. They were proud to have him as their guest. Knowing him, they had no reason to believe that Sir Francis Bacon had anything to do with the plays. Had they foreseen the confusion or words and arguments tha should revolve around this subject centuries later they would have been amazed.

William Oldys in his "Choice Notes," privately printed, says: "Young William D'Avenant was then a little schoolboy in the town, of about seven or eight years old, and so fond also of Shakespeare, that, whenever he heard of his arrival, he would fly from school to see him. One day an old townsman observing the boy running homeward, almost out of breath, asked him whither he was posting in that heat and hurry. He answered, to see his godfather, Shakespeare.

" 'There's a good boy,' said the other, 'but have a care that you don't take God's name in vain.' This story Mr. Pope told me at the Earl of Oxford's table, upon occasion of some discourse which arose about Shakespeare's monument, then newly erected in Westminster Abbey; and he quoted Mr. Betterton, the player as his authority. I answered, that I thought such a story might have enriched the variety of those choice fruits of observation he has presented us in his preface to the edition of our poets works."

I believe that D'Avenant's claim to being the son of Shakespeare was made with his tongue in his cheek. His wish stimulated his avowal. But that Shakespeare was interested in young William's education there can be no denying, and it was this early association that imbued him with the desire to write. Shakespeare, who has influenced literature for all time, found it comparatively simple to direct the mind of one small boy. Thus, though

[183]

there is conjecture as to the possibility of his being the natural father of D'Avenant, there can be no doubt that he was responsible for his intellect. Our minds are nurtured by association with the great. And even though he may not have been the son of Shakespeare, he was warmed by the sun of Shakespeare's genius. No hero could have been more steadfastly worshipped. When Shakespeare died, William D'Avenant wrote his first poem. It was called, *An Ode in Remembrance of Master William Shakespeare.* He was ten years old at the time. It was not however published until 1638 after he had written eight or nine plays and was undoubtedly rewritten many times before it saw print which accounts for its excellence.

2

William D'Avenant attended grammar school in the Parish of All Saints, Oxford, and in 1621 entered as a student in Lincoln's College. That same year his father was elected Mayor of Oxford. Some idea may be had of the high esteem in which he was held in the community when it is known that he did not seek honour, rather was it thrust upon him. The fact that his father was made Mayor of the city is one of the strongest arguments against the premise that William D'Avenant was Shakespeare's son. Had there been even a breath of scandal about his mother, the townsfolk would have turned away from the family rather than affording them the greatest honour it was in their power to bestow. However, Mayor D'Avenant did not enjoy his position long for during that same year his wife died and he was only able to endure life for fourteen days without her. Within two weeks of his wife's death he was buried beside her. Seven children survived, four sons, Robert, William, Nicholas and George and three beautiful daughters whose names I have been unable to discover. William D'Avenant was left one hundred and fifty pounds by his father's will. Each of his brothers received a like amount. The sisters received two hundred pounds each. John D'Avenant left to his son, Nick, his house "at the White Beare in Dettford, which is let to Mr. Harris, schoolmaster of Merchant Tailor's School." To his son Robert, a "Seal-ring." And for the better provision of his family, "My will is that my house shall be left still as a taverne, and supplied with wines continually, for the bringing up and entertainment of my children, until such time as Thomas Hallon, my servant, comes out of his years, and the yearly profitt thereof, necessary expenses of rent, reparacions, and housekeeping being deducted, to returne at the time of his coming forth of his years to my seaven children in equal portions, together with the stock in the cellar, and the debtis, or to the survivors if any happen to die in the meantime."

Of his son William, he says, "My will is also that my sonne, William, being now arrived sixteen years of age, shall be put to prentice to some good merchant of London or other tradesman by the consent and advice of my overseers."

Noble sentiments, but unfortunately, his son, Wil-

[185]

liam, didn't wish the advice of anyone. Therefore he did not finish his course at Lincoln's College but went off to London to seek his fortune. After enjoying the sights of London, he became a page to Frances, Duchess of Richmond. He was at the time a handsome youth, well-spoken, refined, with a ready wit; a born gallant, who charmed with the music of his words. He was somewhat of a scoundrel as well, much interested in affairs of the heart, a fact which was perhaps not unknown to the ladies of London society. Later he was a retainer in the family of Sir Falk Greville, Lord Brook, who was assassinated in 1628. Thereupon D'Avenant commenced writing for the stage, not because he was out of funds, but because he was succumbing to the urge to write. The scourge of genius was upon him. The following year he produced *Alborine, King of Lombardy*, which met with considerable success. During the next ten years he devoted himself almost exclusively to writing. Some of his plays were as follows:

> *The Colonel* July 22, 1629
> *Just Italian* October 2, 1629
> *The Wits* January 19, 1634
> *Love and Honour* November 20, 1634
> *News from Plymouth* August 1, 1635
> *Platonic Lovers* November 16, 1635
> *Unfortunate Lover* April 16, 1638
> *Fair Favourite* November 17, 1638
> *Spanish Lovers* November 30, 1639

He also devised the following Masques for the Court:

The Temple of Love 1634
Triumphs of the Prince D'Amour 1635
Britania Triumphant 1637
Salmacida Spolia 1639

William D'Avenant stood in great favour with the Queen and undoubtedly due to her influence he was made Poet Laureate on the death of Ben Jonson in 1637. D'Avenant was always loyal to the King in disputes between the King and Parliament. In May 1641 he was accused by the Parliament of being connected with a design for seducing the army from its adherence to parliamentary authority and a proclamation was issued for his apprehension. He was arrested at Feversham, sent up to London and placed in the custody of the sergeant at arms. Bail was arranged for him and he fled to France where he sought refuge for a time. It was during this sojourn in France that, as a result of a too arduous amour, he lost his nose. His friends spread the story about that he had lost it honorably in a duel. Others less charitably inclined spread different versions. One wit declared, "If he had not lost his head, he would not have lost his nose." However, words were a sorry ointment that could do but little good. The fact remained that Sir William was minus a nose which caused him considerable annoyance, besides making him a butt for coarse jokes. The humor of the day was seldom salted with refinement. Too frequently we take our noses for granted, but now, alas, poor D'Avenant wasn't able to take his for anything. No longer did he present a comely appearance. His great loss, however, even though it spoiled the symmetry of his profile, could not long dampen his spirits. His enthusiasm and exuberant spirits flowed on unchecked.

But though Sir William to some extent forgot his loss, others could not so easily for they were constantly reminded of it.

Even Sir John Suckling, one of his greatest friends, could not refrain from writing about it. In his *Session of the Poets,* he says:

"Will D'Avenant, ashamed of a foolish mischance,
 That he had got lately travelling in France,
 Modestly hop'd the handsomeness of's Muse
 Might any deformity about him excuse."

And again:

"Surely the company would have been content,
 If they could have found any precedent.
 But in all their records, in verse or prose,
 There was not one laureate *without a nose."*

2

Upon his return to England from France, D'Avenant became a lieutenant-general of ordnance in the army of the Marquis of Newcastle. In France he had been instrumental in getting certain stores into England which the Marquis badly needed. In return, as a mark of appreciation, he was entertained by his lordship. In his military capacity he conducted himself with so much bravery at the siege of Gloucester in 1643 that the King conferred on him the honour of Knighthood. At the final overthrow of the royalists he again fled to France where he entered the Catholic religion, and remained for a considerable time with the Queen and Prince of Wales. She deputed him in the summer of 1646 to urge the King's compliance with certain temporizing measures, but he behaved himself so impertinently, that King Charles I dismissed him with severe exprobation. Returning to Paris he started writing *Gondibert: An Heroick Poem.*

In 1650 he collected a body of artifices together, especially weavers, and set sail from one of the ports in Normandy, for Virginia, the aim being improvement of the Colony. In this enterprise he was encouraged by the Queen-mother. The enterprise, however, was not very fortunate for the vessel was intercepted and D'Avenant was thrown into prison in Cowes Castle, on the Isle of Wight where he continued to write his epic poem. Before he had finished, he was removed to the Tower of London, in order to be tried by the High Commission Court. For awhile the authorities toyed with the idea of removing his head, while William toyed unperturbed with his pen. He was a man without fear, without a nose and stood an excellence chance of eventually being without a head. Nevertheless, he escaped trial, how nobody definitely knows but credit for his rescue is usually given

[189]

to John Milton and two Aldermen of York whom he had permitted to escape from imprisonment when he was Lieutenant-General of Ordnance. Milton at this time, was a man of great influence, and it is not hard to believe that he should have been in sympathy with a poet of such great attainments as D'Avenant. To make a scenario worthy of Hollywood, ten years later, their positions were exactly reversed. Milton found himself in danger of being blacked out. Then D'Avenant came to his rescue and repaid his debt.

But to return to D'Avenant. After his release he commenced looking round for something to do. London was in a rather sorry state as far as the theatre was concerned. Plays by this time had been absolutely prohibited, but nothing daunted and with abundant courage, D'Avenant devised the happy expedient of calling regular dramas, in five acts, entertainments instead of plays. This was the only thing that prevented his liberation from being a change from imprisonment to pauperism. This puritanical aspect toward the theatre was what prompted P. T. Barnum several centuries later to call his enterprise a Museum and not a theatre. People had no hesitancy in visiting Museums for the word sounded so genteel and cultured. And so it was with the attractions of D'Avenant. His *Forest Day's Entertainment* at Rutland House, May 22nd, 1656 was indeed, a mixture of declamation and music, but the eight performances that succeeded,— *The Siege of Rhodes, 1656—The Cruelty of the Spaniards in Peru, 1658—The History of Sir Francis Drake*

1659—*The Fair Favourite*—*Law Against Lovers*—*Playhouse to Be Let*—*The Siege and the Distresses*—were as naughty plays as could have violated the law.

It may be noted here that to D'Avenant must go the credit for producing the first English opera, *The Siege of Rhodes,* mentioned above.

Immediately after the Restoration of King Charles II, however, the stage in London once more commenced to flourish and now it swung to the other extreme. Liberty was unrestrained. The plays overstepped the borderline of decency. The reaction after repression was like a tidal wave. Always the man of the moment, Sir William D'Avenant obtained a patent for the representation of dramatic pieces, under the title of the Duke's Theatre, in Lincoln's Inn Fields. The first presentation was *The Siege of Rhodes* which had ceased miraculously to be merely an entertainment. It was quite an auspicious showing for he used back-drops that were more elaborate than anything shown on the stage heretofore. He used also other stage decorations, flowers and tapestries, suggested by plays he had witnessed in France. A leading man in this company was Thomas Betterton. And now for the first time in the history of the theatre a woman appears upon the stage. Her name, Mary Saunderson.

And it was Sir William D'Avenant who obtained from King Charles II, the Charter under which the National Theatre of Drury Lane still exists. The first playhouse in Drury Lane was built by D'Avenant in the year 1663. It was erected on the site of the old Cock-pit. The King's company removed there and commenced performances on the 8th of April, 1663, with Beaumont and Fletcher's *Humorous Lieutenant* which was acted twelve times successively. And so for the next five years D'Avenant continued with his company. In all, he wrote about thirty plays and made a good deal of money. He altered *Macbeth* to suit his stage and with John Dryden he remodelled *The Tempest*. This was his last performance and it is fitting that it should have been for his whole life was tempestuous. He died in his house in Little Lincoln Inn Fields, April 7th 1668. He was buried in Westminster Abbey under a stone inscribed, like Jonson's, with: "O Rare Sir William D'Avenant."

3

In Pepy's Diary for April 9th 1668, appears the following notation: "I up, and down to the Duke of York's playhouse, there to see, which I did, Sir William D'Avenant's corpse carried out toward Westminster, there to be buried. Here were many coaches and six horses, and many hacknies, that made it look methought, as if it were the buriall of a poor poet. He seemed to have many children, by five or six in the first mourning coach, all boys."

William D'Avenant was twice married. Little, however, is known of his first wife. He left no will but his widow, Mary D'Avenant, administered the estate. She also edited his works and presented them in one volume *Printed in London 1673 By T. N. for Henry Herring*

[192]

Io. Grenhill pinx. W. Faithorne Sculp.

Sir William D'avenant K.

SIR WILLIAM D'AVENANT

THOMAS BETTERTON

man, at the Sign of the Blue Anchor in the Lower Walk of the New Exchange.

The dedication of the book, reads as follows: "To His Royal Highness: Your Highness is no sooner returned from exposing your person for the honour and safety of these kingdoms, but you are persecuted by a poor widow, who humbly begs you to protect the works of her deceased husband from the envy and malice of this censorious age. For whoever sees your Royal Highness's name in the front of this book, and dares oppose what you are pleased to defend, not only shews his weakness, but ill-nature too.

"I have often heard, and I have some reason to believe, that your Royal father, of ever blessed memory, was not displeased with his writings; that your most excellent mother did graciously take him into her family; that she was often diverted by him, and as often smiled upon his endeavours. I am sure he made it the whole study, and labour of the latter part of his life, to entertain his Majesty and his Royal Highness, and I hope he did it successfully.

"Whenever we are, or whenever we fear to be opprest, we always fly to Your Highness for redress or prevention, and you were ever graciously pleased to protect us. 'Tis that has emboldened me to present these papers to your Royal Highness, and I humbly beg pardon for the presumption of your most humble and obedient servant: Mary D'Avenant."

[193]

The dedication to: "His Royal Highness," referred, of course, to the Duke of York, afterwards James II.

4

Sir Walter Scott said of him: "Sir William D'Avenant, made a meritorious, though misguided and unsuccessful effort to rescue poetry from becoming a mere hand-maid of pleasure, or the partisan of political or personal disputes, and to restore her to her natural rank in society, as an auxiliary of religion, poetry, law and virtue. His heroic poem of *Gondibert,* has, no doubt, great imperfections; but it intimates everywhere a mind above those laborious triflers, who called that *poetry* which was only *verse,* and very often exhibits a majestic, dignified, and manly simplicity, equally superior to the metaphysical school, by the doctrines of which D'Avenant was occasionally misled. Yet, if that author too frequently immitated their quaint affectations of uncommon sentiment and associations, he had at least the merit of couching them in stately and harmonious verse; a quality of poetry totally neglected by the followers of Cowley. I mention D'Avenant here, and separate from the other poets, who were distinguished about the time of the Restoration because I think that Dryden was at that period, an admirer and imitator of *Gondibert,* as we are certain that he was a personal and intimate friend of the author."

5

And of D'Avenant, John Dryden has written: " found him of so quick a fancy, that nothing was propose to him on which he could not suddenly produce a thought extremely pleasant and surprising; and those first thoughts of his, contrary to the old Latin proverb, were not always the least happy; and as his fancy was quick, so likewise were the products of it remote and new. He borrowed not of any other; and his imaginations were such as could not easily enter into any other man. His corrections were sober and judicious, and he corrected his own writings much more severely than those of another man; bestowing twice the time and labour in polishing which he used in invention."

6

But perhaps nobody summed up the work of Sir William D'Avenant more simply and concisely than he did himself, when he wrote, in his introduction to *Gondibert:* "I'll only tell you my endeavour was in bringing truth, too often absent, home to men's bosoms, to lead her through unfrequented and new ways, and from the most remote shades, by representing nature, though not in an affected, yet in an unusual dress."

After his death D'Avenant slipped into a state bordering on oblivion for two hundred years. Then once more his genius slowly began to be recognized. But his fame has grown dim beside the figure of lesser men, which is strange. Once he declared Homer unworthy of imitation; now there is nobody who imitates *him*. One of his contemporaries declared that it was his ambition to be rare, and his misfortune to be successful. Nevertheless,

[195]

no student of theatrical history can fail to agree that he was thoroughly original, a writer who carved new paths. Therefore it is all the more droll to realize, that he who in life was the most original of poets, in death is commemorated by an epitaph borrowed from the grave of another poet:

"O Rare Ben Jonson."
"O Rare Sir William D'Avenant."

15

THOMAS BETTERTON

ACCORDING TO Colley Cibber, Thomas Betterton, actor
and gentleman, like Shakespeare was without even a
serious competitor. "The most Vandyke can arrive at is
to make his portraits of great persons seem to think. A
Shakespeare goes farther, and tells what his picture
thought. A Betterton steps beyond them both, and calls
them from the grave to breathe and be themselves again
in feature, speech and motion."

Colley Cibber was one of the greatest commentators
of his time, second only to Pepys in his vivid thumb-nail
portraiture.

It is too bad there were no motion pictures in those
days to record the superb acting of such men as Garrick,
Betterton, Macklin, Barry, Quin, Mossop and a few
others. How marvelous it would be today if we could sit
in Radio City Music Hall and behold all those celebrated actors in performances as they actually took place.
Through the printed page, Shakespeare, Jonson and
Sheridan have been preserved to us until we are so familiar with them they almost seem like contemporaries.
But the good acting a man does, lives after him only in
the memories of those who knew him, later only by hear-
say and tradition, until eventually they become legends.

At least that is the way it was during the times of which I am writing.

Thomas Betterton was born in 1635 in Tothill Street, Westminster, a fairly respectable neighborhood at the time, since not long afterwards, "The Master of the Revels," whose duty it was to control the British drama, took up residence there. The elder Betterton was a cook in the Royal household of King Charles I. Perhaps his position made him ambitious for he wished his boy to grow up to be a well-educated gentleman. Care was taken of his formative years. He was furnished with good teachers. When later he showed an aptitude toward literature, he was apprenticed to John Rhodes, the Charing Cross bookseller. Rhodes had been wardrobe-keeper to the theatre in Black Friars before opening his bookshop. He had been exposed to contagion, and now the lure of the theatre was hopelessly in his blood. He could no more keep away from the stage than a criminal can keep away from the place of his crime. Therefore in 1659 he secured a licence to get together a company of players to act at the Cockpit in Drury Lane. This theatre, sometimes called the Phoenix, had a lowly origin. It began as a place where cock-fights were held and later gave way to becoming a full-fledged theatre. Nevertheless I cannot believe that it was anything but a shabby, tawdry place. Certainly in its early days it was not held in very high repute and puritanical souls were constantly clamoring for its destruction. Fortunately all their verbal outbursts came to naught, for it was here that Thomas Betterton

[198]

first acted, inasmuch as he had enrolled himself as a member of the Rhodes' company. It took very little experience to make him proficient, a master in every part he attempted. In the course of his subsequent long career on the stage, he included in his repertoire more than a hundred and thirty difficult rôles. The place which Betterton holds in dramatic history is no small one, for he gave dignity to the drama after the Restoration at a time when the theatre stood badly in need of a leader. Before Betterton's time most players in the supporting casts were rogues or vagabonds. To eke out their miserable existence they took jobs at whatever they could do, usually at the most menial labor, as servants, stable-boys or farm-hands.

Betterton lifted acting out of chaos even as Shake-speare had performed the same service for the drama. He was celebrated for the perfection of his manners, his scholarship and the force of his intellect. As a player he was without parallel in his time. He played *Hamlet* and *Othello* even better than Garrick, a fact which few writers dispute but he was not as versatile as Garrick. He could not turn as quickly from tragedy to comedy. Garrick frequently did this by acting two dissimilar plays on the same evening. Nor could Betterton dance with astounding grace. The dignity of Betterton was blended with tenderness. He read his parts as though he knew what the author intended. His face was expressive, his voice powerful. He spoke with an authority suited to his characters. He was a master of moods, mild, grand, sad

[199]

or gay. His acting was illuminated; tipped in stardust and in the warmth of the sun.

A contemporary actor, Anthony Aston, has left an admirable portrait of Betterton among his writings. I am quoting it here because it is so different from the picture our minds conjure up.

"Mr. Betterton, although a superlative good actor, labored under an ill figure, being clumsily made, having a great head, a short thick neck, stooped in the shoulders, and had fat short arms, which he rarely lifted higher than his stomach. His left hand frequently lodged in his breast, between his coat and waistcoat, while with his right he prepared his speech. His actions were few, but just. He had little eyes and a broad face, a little pock-fretten, a corpulent body and thick legs, with large feet. He was better to meet than to follow; for his aspect was serious, venerable, and majestic; in his latter time a little paralytic. His voice was low and grumbling; yet he could tune it by an artificial climax, which enforced universal attention, even from the fops and orange-girls. He was incapable of dancing, even in a country dance; as was Mrs. Barry; but their good qualities were more than equal to their deficiencies."

And yet despite so many apparent defects, his very presence commanded attention. Most playgoers are critics. Each thinks the best he has seen is the best that ever existed. And so it was that Colley Cibber declared that all actors fell short of Betterton. But then Mr. Cibber's opinion was not without prejudice for there were several renowned artists of the day who had aroused his displeasure. Nevertheless it is generally conceded that Betterton's Falstaff has never been surpassed.

In 1661 Betterton was a leading actor in the Duke's Company under the distinguished management of Sir William D'Avenant. Betterton played *Hamlet,* changed as was the custom to meet what was imagined to be the taste of the time. It is also ineresting to note that he enacted the part of Mercutio in a version of *Romeo and Juliet* that had a happy ending. A few years after D'Avenant's death, Betterton assumed management of the company.

Thomas Betterton was truly well-favored by the gods in many ways. His wife, Mary Saunderson, also an actress was a veritable genius in the art of living. She spurred him on to ever greater and greater achievements. Few marriages have been happier than theirs. They were married in 1670. She remained the leading lady of his company until her retirement in 1693. The story of their married life is one of tenderness and deepest devotion. They conquered age by growing old gracefully together. Age at best is but a comparative term, a cloak that doesn't exist unless you permit it to fall about your shoulders.

Betterton was the first actor to ever use movable scenery in place of the tapestry back-drop which had hitherto been the custom. Crude though the scenery undoubtedly was, it led the way for the magnificent spectacles and stage effects of the present day.

[201]

There is little material whereof to weave a biography of Betterton and though several have attempted it, nobody sums up his career more capably than Samuel Pepys, writing in his diary in October 1662, almost half a century before the great actor's death in 1710: "He is a very sober, serious man and studious, and humble, following of his studies; and is rich already with what he gets and saves."

Pepys might have added that "what he gets" wasn't very much. His highest salary was not in excess of six pounds per week, while his wife after her retirement received the generous pension of one pound per week. Nevertheless, Betterton was occasionally made grants by men who were devoted to the drama and held him in esteem, and there is no doubt that after his final retirement, he passed his remaining days in comparative comfort.

Betterton always liked to act to a silent house. He cared little for wild outbursts of applause. What he wished was to evoke wrapt attention. To arouse a house, he considered comparatively easy; to subdue it was an accomplishment.

16

PEEPS AT GARRICK

THE OTHER day I was browsing through a book by Thomas Davies entitled *Memoirs of the Life of David Garrick, Esq., interspersed with Characters and Anecdotes of His Theatrical Contemporaries, the whole forming A History of The Stage which includes a Period of Thirty-Six Years.* With such a title it is not to be wondered at that the *Memoirs* are in two volumes. They were published in 1780 in London. The book bears the following inscription, "Printed for the Author, and sold at his Shop in Great Russell Street, Covent-Garden."

In one of the books which by the way bears the book plate of Charles T. Congdon, there is pasted a newspaper clipping. It reads as follows, "Davies, Thomas, a bookseller and writer, was brought up at Edinburgh, and in 1736 became an actor at the Haymarket theatre. He afterward turned bookseller, but not succeeding in that line, turned strolling player. About 1762 he commenced bookselling again in Russell Street Covent-Garden, but in 1778 he became bankrupt, and was relieved by the exertions of Dr. Johnson. In 1780 he published the *Life of Garrick* which had a good sale. He also wrote *Dramatic Miscellanies;* the *Life of Henderson the Player;* and several fugitive pieces. He died in 1785."

All this by way of preamble, to what I set out to write.

[203]

I have always been very interested in the marginal notes often to be found in books, comments and notations. I know of one instance where an author wrote a complete story centering around the marginal notes he found in the books in a library he was privileged to examine. There is so much that books could tell if only they could speak.

In any event, while I was reading Davies' *Garrick* several slips of paper fell out and fluttered to the floor. They were clippings about David Garrick clipped from an old newspaper, perhaps by Charles T. Congdon. They were so old they were almost falling to dust. There was no indication of the name of the newspaper. I imagine it must have been printed a century ago, or even longer. The article was headed, *Account of Garrick, In a letter from a Gentleman to his Friend in Germany, dated London, 1768, Communicated by B. Thompson, Jun., Esq.* The article is incomplete but nevertheless I have decided to quote it here in the hope that it may interest others as much as it interested me.

"I yesterday spent one of the pleasantest days of my life at Garrick's country-house. I left London early, in company with Murphy; it was a voluptuous summer's morning: a transparent mist trembled through the warm expanse, as in Claude Loraine's landscapes, and nature gained additional beauty through its veil; I felt as if borne on ether—happiness smiled all around me.

"Garrick's house is a little palace, and built in good proportion; it is situated on the banks of the Thames which there winds through a well-inhabited and richly cultivated country; but, what is called his garden, is nothing more than a large grass-plat, kept in good order, on which are scattered, without symmetry, various bushes and interwoven trees; Horace describes a place like this, in the third ode of his second book,

'Quà pinus ingens, albaque populus
Umbram hospitalem consociare amant
Ramis; & obliquo laborat
Lympha fugax trepidare rivo.'

Near the water stands the temple of Shakespeare, a sanctuary to every Briton, in the strictest sense of the word. The statue, erected to the memory of the immortal bard, is of white marble, and as large as life. The sculptor has succeeded most happily: he has given him a look of enchantment, as if he were wandering in worlds of his own creation, and listening to the song of Ariel.

"In the house neither magnificence nor fashion are to be discovered; but, instead of these, a pleasing, noble simplicity, which seems to belong to a country life; and here and there marks of the genius, as well as the disposition of the owner. All the rooms are light and agreeable to the eye; they are ornamented with pictures of celebrated actors and actresses, in principal scenes, which are well executed. There are four remarkable pictures, by Hogarth, the originals of his election; but a fifth is still more so; it is meant as a counterpart to his *Marriage à la Mode;* and to represent, in four pictures, a really happy marriage; but, either nature has been too scanty of—"

Here the clipping is torn and several paragraphs are missing. Probably they are the most interesting of all. Nevertheless, the account as I have found it, continues as follows: "I have now heard, from Garrick himself, a confirmation of the story relative to the likeness of Fielding, prefixed to Murphy's edition of his works. Hogarth drew it, from memory, after Fielding's death; and being unable to call to mind a remarkable turn of the mouth, Garrick imitated it, and thereby refreshed Hogarth's imagination. This reminds me of an anecdote, respecting Garrick, at Rome.—In a society of artists, the conversation turned on the expression of the passions, when Garrick rose, and exhibited them, individually, with dreadful exactness. I have myself seen something of this kind, in his repetition of a short piece, wherein he had no character, yet represented every part, even those of the women, to the performers, with incredible minuteness. It is unaccountable how a texture of nerves, so finely woven, can bear so constant a distension, without a total destruction of his health; for you must not suppose that the storm of passions only affects his surface. I saw him once, after having played the part of Richard, stretched, like the expiring Germanicus in Poussin's picture, on a sofa, panting, pale, speechless, covered with perspiration, and unable to raise his arm.

"In the country, Garrick regains his exhausted faculties, and he flies from town whenever he can catch an open day. 'Then,' says he, 'I enjoy an hour or two of my life; in town, I belong to the nation.' Not only his arduous application, but also the government of the theatre, often robs him of peace and comfort. This government partakes of all the inconveniences, which attach to the British constitution. At one time, a storm arises in the House of Commons, or Green Room; at another, their lordships, the authors, are dissatisfied;

> Who with a play, like pistol cock'd in hand,
> Bid managers to stand,
> 'Deliver, Sir,
> Your thoughts on this.'
> 'But Madam,—Miss—'
> 'Your answer straight,
> I will not wait.'
> ' 'Tis fit you know—'
> 'I'll hear no reason:
> This very season,
> Aye or no.'

   "The voice of the people is terrible; for, as in Athens, when out of humour, the greatest cannot escape its censure. Garrick, indeed, is a great favorite, and generally suits the taste of rigid judges; yet he acknowledges their dominion with humility, and knows that they never forgive a fault—or even a neglect. Nor is he insensible to the sarcasms of solitary critics; and, like all other meritorious men, has not escaped the cabals of envy, and the shafts of calumny. Indignation at such treatment was, in

[207]

part, the cause of his long journey through foreign countries. He described his sensations at that period in the
following lines;

'The looking up fatigues the sight,
And mortals, when they soar,
Should they once reach a certain height,
All wish to have them low'r.
And friends there are in this good town,
Will lend a hand to help them down.'

"Garrick does not deserve such treatment. He has
never been an enemy to genius; never humbled opening
talent by contempt. He has often drawn forth unknown
perfections, always valued and rewarded exertion and
shared reputation, as well as emolument, with his associates. He is not only the instructor, but the father of
his company, and reveres rare endowment with enthusiasm. After Mrs. Prichard had left the stage, he gave her
an annual benefit; always acted, and often wrote a little
piece for the occasion. He still speaks of the memorable
Mrs. Cibber, in terms of warm sensibility. 'She felt,' says
he, 'and made all others feel. Since her death I have not
been able to perform the part of a lover.' True it is, his
services are most bounteously rewarded. His fortune i
valued at £100,000, and the theatre produces for him, a
performer and joint proprietor, £4,000 more per an
num. If wealth, understanding, and fame can make
man happy, Garrick must be happy; and, in his ow
house, he is so; for his wife is an amiable, charmin

DAVID GARRICK

COLLEY CIBBER

woman, who retains nothing of her former situation, except—grace; but they are not blessed with children, the comfort and solace of age. Garrick's fortune will, therefore, fall to the lot of his brother's family. As he is to play next week, his desk was covered with petitions for places from ladies and gentlemen of all ranks. There was a foreign prince among the supplicants, and a British minister. It was no wonder if a man, so universally idolized, should, at last, become proud. Baron was so with far less right. Garrick, however, assumes no dignity, but to fools, whose harassing solicitations can only be answered by coldness.

"It is impossible that a picture of Garrick, in one character, can be like him in another; for the soul of this Proteus always clothes itself in a new body. He who has seen him in Lear and Richard, does not know the individual Garrick. Hogarth's Richard, which so admirably expresses the spirit of the character, is not like Garrick even on the stage. In the Hamlet of Zoffanij, except the attitude, I cannot discover a trace of him; but the same artist has painted him better in Romeo, at the moment when Juliet awakes. Reynolds' poetical painting, in which Garrick is standing between the tragic and comic muse, like Hercules, at the double path, and with more humanity than the demi-god, decrees in favour of the laughter-loving maid, is a masterpiece. In the eye, as well as in the arch smile, is truth; but yet the Vandykish regulations of the drapery and hair, advantageous as it was to the artist, throws a kind of foreign cast upon the painting. A painter from Bath, (whose name I forget), has drawn him as large as life, in the act of embracing Shakespeare's statue. The thought is not a happy one, and the artist is not one of the first in England; but Garrick is discoverable enough. Colman has the best picture of him. It is a profile, painted by Zoffanij. This position of the face is always nearer to the line of truth, and expresses the character of the countenance more decisively. On my return, I alighted, for a moment, to see Pope's garden at Twickenham, which is remarkable for nothing but his name. The so-highly extolled grotto is nothing more than an indifferent cavern, tastelessly loaded with shells, in which, here and there, a little water trickles down."

So ends the portrait of David Garrick as one of his contemporaries knew him.

17

CHARLES MACKLIN

1

ON FEBRUARY 15th, 1741, Charles Macklin played the part of Shylock for the first time and thereby made theatrical history. For many years prior to that date, *The Merchant of Venice* had been presented not as Shakespeare wrote it but in a vulgarized form known as *The Jew of Venice*. This atrocious concoction had been the work of Lord Lansdowne who blandly imagined that he could improve on Shakespeare's original rendering. Such an attempt was as absurd as though an art student attempted to improve on the work of Rembrandt or Raphael. Historians state that his Lordship took great pains to preserve regularity in the alteration, but in so doing, they admit, he greatly enervated the drama that he meant to improve. In *The Jew of Venice* the part of Shylock was relegated to one of the least important characters in the play instead of one of the most prominent as Shakespeare intended. He was always played by a very low comedian. Charles Macklin knew that *The Jew of Venice* was not the Shylock of Shakespeare, and so on that momentous occasion when he persuaded Fleetwood to revive *The Merchant of Venice* he made theatrical history.

I quote from the *Memoirs of James Thomas Kirkman,*

[211]

of the Honorable Society of Lincoln's Inn, Macklin's biographer and friend. "During the rehearsal of the play, Mr. Macklin did not let any person, not even the players, see how he intended to act the part. He merely repeated the lines of the character, and did not by so much as one single look, tone, gesture, or attitude disclose his manner of personating this cruel Israelite. The actors declared that Macklin would spoil the performance; and Mr. Quin went so far as to say, that he would be hissed off the stage, for his arrogance and presumption. Nay, even the manager himself expostulated with him, concerning the propriety of his persevering in his intention of having *The Merchant of Venice* represented, in opposition to the judgement of so eminent a personage, as Lord Lansdowne; to the opinion of Mr. Quin and the rest of the actors; and, indeed, to the voice of the public, who had so often testified their approbation of the noble Lord's play. Thus did Mr. Fleetwood argue with Macklin, and strenuously urge him to abandon his resolution. His character as an actor, might, he said, be materially injured by a perseverance in his determination, and ultimately by a failure in the performance of the part; but Mr. Macklin, supported throughout by his sound sense and acute discrimination, continued firm to his purpose, and had *The Merchant of Venice* announced for representation, on the 14th of February 1741."

Whether Macklin was right or wrong in his attitude nobody knew at the moment, although the consensus of opinion was against him, but of one thing there can be no shadow of a doubt. The arguments pro and con were so vociferous behind the scenes that most of the actors were pitched to a high tension of anticipation. It seemed incredible that the famous Mr. Quin who was to act the part of Antonio could be wrong in his opinions. Quin was looked upon as a theatrical oracle who was practically infallible. In promoting the play excellent press-agent work must have been done; although such a term was unknown in those days, for on that opening night the house was quickly crowded in every section. The audience was a motley one. Some had come to jeer, some to cheer. But all were keenly interested whether they came to support the act or merely to appease their curiosity.

I can imagine with what enthusiasm Charles Macklin walked about behind the scenes that night. What strange emotions surged through him as he awaited the rising of the curtain? Did he perhaps dream that that night he would portray a rôle that would live deathlessly for two hundred years, one of the most robust of portrayals the English stage had ever seen, a Shylock that would never be equalled again save once, by the immortal Edmund Kean. Kean too was to feel exactly the same about Shylock as did Macklin. And Kean too made a further innovation for he played Shylock without the atrocious red wig of Lansdowne's Shylock whereas Macklin had retained the red wig.

Before the curtain rose that night, the Manager, Mr. Fleetwood strode about the Green Room in great distress. How badly he needed an aspirin I can well imagine. He hoped that Macklin's impending oblivion would not spread out to engulf him. Meanwhile to add to Macklin's nervousness, the other actors and actresses indulged in jokes and jabs and jibes at his discomfiture. After all he wasn't worth considering. He was about to make his exit from the stage. Who was he that he imagined that he could belittle the work of the mighty Lord Lansdowne and survive? I wonder if the shade of Shakespeare sat in the pit that night, smiling gently, and musing over the reflection that on a certain day and in the days of centuries to come his own dramatic efforts would not be deemed without merit.

In my mind's eye I can see Macklin now walking up to the curtain and gazing through the eye-hole at the multitudes waiting impatiently for the play to begin. And I can hear him turn and say, "Good! Tonight I shall be tried by a special jury."

And then the curtain rises and the play begins. Nothing untoward happened. The first entrances were received with the usual apathy on the part of the audience. When Shylock and Bassanio, who was played by Mr. Millward, entered in the third scene, they were greeted by a silence so intense that the theatre might almost have been empty. It was as though every person in that audience were poised to spring, to tear down a god or to create a new one, according to the shift of the wind. Afterward Mr. Macklin declared that the coolness shown by the audience at that moment, the lack of friendliness, affected him more than anything that had happened that night. He was indeed on trial before a jury, a cold, calculating, merciless jury eager to condemn. He must show rare eloquence in his plea if he were to be acquitted. Bear in mind that for years he had been a great favorite among the playgoers of the town and his entrances were usually the occasion for an outburst of applause. Tonight there was none. Not a hand clapped encouragement. Nothing material was apparent to put him at his ease. And before him were all those eyes watching intently for the slightest error in diction or a false note in inflection. Nor did Mr. Fleetwood with his terrified expression serve any worthy purpose. Nor the actors with their malicious sneers. They seemed to be licking their lips, waiting for the kill. How pleasant it is to watch the mighty fall. It is like visting the home of a sick friend so that we may strut about before him and impress him with the quantity of our excellent health. And yet despite everything, Macklin would not be confounded. He would not be dismayed. And perhaps it was because he had ceased to be Charles Macklin, he was in truth Shylock, cold, aloof, contemptuous but withal proud because he was a Jew.

And so the play moved logically onward. The audience scarcely moved. Not a sound rippled over that auditorium and while it is true there was no applause, it is also true that there ceased to be sneers. In spite of themselves they were moved by the magic of acting such as they had never beheld before.

[215]

Macklin's acting had always been noted for its naturalness. His was no affectation, no exaggeration, no absurd
declamation, no shouting to the gallery for approval.
Although he lived two hundred years ago his manner-
isms were such as are used today by the greatest of our
actors, although few of them have ever approached his
completeness of portrayal. For Macklin became the characters he assailed. And so he played Shylock with all the
countless changing shades of character—the malevolence,
the villainy, the tragedy and pathos, but above all the
bitterness and frustration. It is doubtful if the personal
triumph of a performer was ever more complete. He
swept all opposition before him. And when the play was
over it was as though the pentup emotions of the audience had been suddenly loosed, as though a dam had
burst and the applause swept out in a mighty flood. Mr.
Fleetwood almost had a heart attack, so acute was his
pleasurable amazement. He had lived to behold a mir-
acle. But through all the storm of triumph, Charles
Macklin stood and smiled calmly as he said, "I am not
worth fifty pounds in the world; nevertheless on this
night I am Charles the Great!"

On the third night of the run of *The Merchant of
Venice,* official seal was placed on the document of his
triumph, for Pope sat in the stage box and declared emphatically, "This is the Jew, that Shakespeare drew."

So decisive was this judgment because of the eminence
of the juror, *The Jew of Venice* as conceived by Lord
Lansdowne vanished into that obscurity from which *The*

Merchant of Venice had once more so dramatically emerged.

2

Great day though that was, another was to come many years later equally as dramatic and certainly as memorable, January 10th 1788, for on that day Macklin stepped upon the stage to once more portray Shylock to an appreciative audience. He was then ninety-eight years old. His health was far from good and had it not been for the insistence of his friends it is doubtful if he would have attempted so arduous a rôle. But the clamor for his appearance was so great and the sincere flattery of his followers so invigorating, he stepped out on the stage exhibiting spirit and vigour. An actor breathes in applause with the same eagerness that he breathes in the air and it filters to every fibre of his body. The house was crowded, not a seat was empty and vast throngs were standing in every available spot. It was a kind audience, that loved the old actor. They gazed on him in awe and the auditorium was tremulous with sympathy and devotion.

Considering his great age, he went through the first act splendidly. Then came the second and his memory commenced to waver. He stood and gazed speechless at the audience. He rubbed his hand wearily across his eyes. Words, words, in his mind they were all jumbled and confused. As through a mist, he looked around him. He couldn't go on. He gasped audibly and made a desperate effort to clear his brain of the fog that was struggling to engulf it. Then by sheer will-power he managed to pull himself together. But the words of the play still evaded him. Fearlessly he faced the dreadful fact, the bane of the life of every actor. His memory was momentarily depleted. Slowly he walked to the edge of the stage. Conscious of his defeat and yet with a composure and solemnity that were inspiring, he said, "Ladies and Gentlemen: Within these very hours I have been seized with a terror of mind I never in my life felt before; it has totally destroyed my corporeal as well as my mental faculties. I must therefore request your patience this night: a request which an old man may hope is not unreasonable. Should it be granted, you may depend that this will be the last night, unless my health shall be entirely re-established, of my ever appearing before you in so ridiculous a situation."

As Mr. Macklin finished speaking, he withdrew and the applause was deafening. Never had he been greeted by such sympathetic outbursts of understanding. It filled every part of the theatre. It touched his heart. It surged to his brain. The fog rolled miraculously away. His memory reasserted itself, a most amazing effect. Shortly afterward he was able to resume the play, and did not again falter in his lines. As the audience left the theatre they knew that they had beheld a performance the like of which they would perhaps never behold again—an old man who had lived almost a century and yet was still able to play on every human emotion. Nevertheless, it was believed that Macklin was through with acting forever. However, this proved far from the case. Necessity drove him back to the stage. At this time the sole amount of his ready cash was sixty pounds. Besides this he had an income of ten pounds per year. In fact so narrow were his circumstances, he was forced once more to return to the theatre for subsistence.

While acting the role of Sir Pertinax MacSycophant, in the *Man of the World* on the 28th of November 1788 he was once more attacked by loss of memory and again he was forced to address the audience. He informed them that unless he found himself more capable, he would never again attempt to act before them. What a pity it was that in Great Britain at that time there was no such organization as "The Actors' Fund" in order that this grand old actor might not have been forced by poverty, ill-health and infirmities of age to struggle onward with impaired intellect. He should have been granted a home somewhere in the country where he could have spent his last years in peace and rest. "However," writes one who knew him personally, "so it was; but Mr. Macklin's mind, like the flashes of an expiring taper, displayed signs of vigour to the very end of his theatrical career."

During the month of February, he acted the part of Shylock and Sir Archy Macfarcalm at Covent-Garden on the same night. Both performances were eminently successful for his memory was excellent. The beholders were astonished at his apparent firmness of tone, but their astonishment increased a few months later when he again played the part of Sir Pertinax MacSycophant in

[219]

the *Man of the World* for this part had a great many speeches that ran almost fifty lines each, yet never once did he falter, despite the fact that he was in his one hundredth year.

His final appearance on the stage was in the part of Shylock, May 7th, 1789, at his own benefit performance. This time however he was not feeling so well. As he sat in the Green Room before the beginning of the play, his mind wandered. Near by, Ryder, an actor of merit, sat, also made up as Shylock, ready to take over, should the old master fail. The manager had taken this precaution because he had a premonition that all might not go well. Ryder was an actor of considerable merit, a great success in Ireland, who had made the foolish gesture of attempting to be his own manager with luckless results. He was glad of the opportunity of playing understudy to Mr. Macklin.

As the failing Macklin sat waiting in the Green Room, Miss Pope approached him.

"Are you going to play tonight?" he asked.

"Why, yes," said she, surprised, "I am playing the rôle of Portia."

Macklin seemed much interested. "And who plays Shylock?"

"Why you, sir," she gasped. "See, you are dressed for it. Do you not remember?"

The thin old hands shook and worked convulsively as though endeavoring to clutch at reality. He seemed much affected. Ryder brought him a glass of water. As he drank eagerly, perhaps he gazed as in a dream at this strange apparition of a second Shylock, confused more than ever, wondering if he were losing his mind. Seemingly he was much affected by the incident. He drew his hand across his eyes, and in a pathetic tone he murmured, "Age, age."

Then he tottered out on the stage. Ryder stood in the wings waiting, waiting his cue, the cue of a stage manager that is merciless—Time. Macklin stood for a moment on the stage, fighting desperately to collect his thoughts. Not by the slightest sound did the audience confuse him. All alone he stood on the threshold of reality, beyond loomed the future, that great grim guess. But before him was an expectant audience. He made one or two fruitless efforts to go on, but it was no use. Sadly, with a catch in his feeble voice, he confessed to the audience that it was impossible. He had done his best. Amid the farewell applause of the multitudes he was led from the stage forever, a broken old man. And Ryder, realizing that his expected cue had come, took over the part and played brilliantly, though I cannot believe that the thoughts of the audience were upon the play, but upon that feeble old man who had had his hour and now was to be heard no more.

3

But though Macklin retired from the stage he could not cut himself off from the theatre completely and hereafter was a frequent visitor at Covent-Garden. And he continued to write and revise plays for presentation.

Particularly did he appear conspicuously in the pit every night when the King visited the theatre, and I can imagine his gratitude when the King acknowledged him as one Sovereign might bow to another. For a moment they met on common ground but with one difference, the Sovereign of the Drama was financially little better than a pauper. Then through the kind offices of a few of his friends, his two plays, the *Man of the World* and *Love à la Mode* were printed under the supervision of a certain Mr. Murphy and offered for public sale by subscription. So great was the public response more than sixteen hundred pounds were made on the transaction. With this amount and under the guidance of some men of finance, annuities were purchased from which Mr. Macklin was to draw two hundred pounds per year for the remainder of his life, while seventy-five pounds per annum were to be paid to Mrs. Elizabeth Macklin, his wife, in the event that she survived him. This arrangement was eminently satisfactory to the old fellow and he brightened up considerably. There were still pleasant years ahead. He had not as yet reached the end of his long earthly journey that he had enjoyed so thoroughly.

Macklin continued to live peacefully, though in constantly failing health and failing memory. Sometimes he was unable to recognize his most intimate friends, but fortunately these moments were of brief duration. But deafness withdrew him further from the happenings of things about him. He could scarcely hear words that were shouted at him. For long hours he used to sit b the window gazing out into the garden, his eyes closed as though he were sleeping. Perhaps in memory he was living over his tangled eventful life. How long ago it was since little Charles M'Laughlin was born of highly respected parents somewhere in Ireland during the month of May in 1690.

He had lived lustily and fought much. He never turned away from a friend or fled from an enemy. His life was a series of skirmishes. Even the parts he wished to play on the stage were attacked with a fury that was never abated until they were conquered. He was possessed of surpassing strength and courage. His uncle had been a Catholic priest who undertook his education and then abandoned it when he discovered that the boy was unruly. Thereafter little effort was made toward giving him an education. Some writers claim that until he was thirty-five he could only read indifferently but I cannot believe this because of the parts he played and in which he was letter-perfect. Great men inspire legends. It is hard to separate the true from the imagined. When he was scarcely eight years old he was acting in private enterprises and it is my belief that even at this early age he was able to read his own parts. A man of Macklin's mentality could scarcely have neglected his reading in so fantastic a manner.

During his life he played many parts, but unfortunately only those behind the footlights did he always play well. In 1710 we find him working as a porter in Trinity College, Dublin. Undoubtedly he was also study-

[223]

ing in his spare time. For five years he was a tramp, strolling about Great Britain and during this period little is known about him. Then in 1725 he appeared as Alcander in *Oedipus* in Lincoln's Inn Fields. His acting was so natural it was not appreciated. So he became a strolling player once more, working occasionally when he could find a part. In 1730 he played at "The Southwark Fair" and then back to Lincoln's Inn Fields. In 1733 he was playing small parts in Drury Lane. His first wife was Grace Purvor whom he met at the home of Barton Booth.

All his life, Charles Macklin struggled constantly to overcome his Irish brogue. This was finally accomplished by the time he played Shylock. Shylock was Macklin's first and greatest success, and somehow it almost seemed as though the part suited him so well it became mixed with his blood.

Charles Macklin was always much more fearful of being exposed than of being misrepresented. He was continually harassed by the prejudices of an illiberal world. He believed that his birth could neither confer credit on him if he did not deserve it, nor withhold it from him if he did. Such is James Thomas Kirkman's estimate of him which appears in his long biography published in 1799

On Tuesday morning, the 11th of July 1797, Charle Macklin died quietly and without pain. His final word were, "Let me go! Let me go!" Prophetic indeed hi words were for his memory has gone on to be preserve

From a drawing by Ramberg, dated 1806.

MACKLIN AS SHYLOCK

TITLE PAGE OF THE FIRST FOLIO

forever in the annals of that small company who make theatrical tradition.

Mr. Macklin's life was stormy and tempestuous. The spirited nature of the Irish was in him. He was forever giving vent to his violent temper and enjoyed a brawl with keen relish. Occasionally such outbursts ended disastrously. One evening in 1735 while he was acting the part of Snip in *The Merry Cobbler* he became embroiled in argument with another actor named Thomas Hallam. Neither of them used any care in their choice of language. And so noisy did they become, they annoyed the other actors who were concluding the first part of the play. The enormous battle being waged was over the theft of a wig. Hallam later returned the wig but Macklin's temper had broken all bounds. Then Hallam made the grave mistake of using such offensive language, that Macklin lunged at him with his cane as though it had been a sword.

With such force was the cane driven, it went through Hallam's left eye and penetrated the brain, inflicting injuries from which he died the following day. Thereupon Macklin was arrested and later charged with murder. His friends rallied around and numerous witnesses appeared in his behalf. So ably did they make their plea, the verdict was manslaughter, since there had been no premeditation. However, it would seem that the conviction was not a very serious one, for shortly thereafter we find him appearing as Ramillie, a part authored by Fielding, amidst great applause.

[225]

Although this was the most serious dispute in Macklin's long career of a hundred and seven years, there were many others. And yet apparently there were never any religious difficulties, for his father was a Presbyterian farmer of Ulster, his mother a devout Roman Catholic, while Charles himself attained immortality as a Jew.

18

MRS. SIDDONS

1

IT IS reported that Mrs. Siddons could quell a London mob by simply saying, "Good people, let me pass; I am Sarah Siddons." Thereupon a path miraculously opened for her sedan chair. No story of any length more surely mirrors her character. She had stirred the imagination of the mob. Even a queen could not have exacted more sincere homage. She was reverenced as much as though she were royal born. Though she was not a queen, her appearance was all that of a queen should be, beautiful, haughty and more. She was hypnotic. She swayed the mob.

Sarah Siddons was born in Brecon, Wales, in 1755. Her father was Roger Kemble, a strolling player. He managed a small company of actors touring through Gloucestershire, Staffordshire and Warwickshire. Her mother was Sarah Ward, daughter of John Ward, a renowned Irish actor. She was a fine-looking woman whose voice was as clear as a bell. She pronounced every word distinctly, so that it fell on the ear like a caress.

Roger Kemble's company had no standing in the eyes of the law. The members of it were vagabonds whose mode of travel was frequently a rout. They were driven from one town to another by the authorities who, however, neglected to provide them with a coach. Food and shelter were luxuries which they were not always in a position to enjoy due to the complete depletion of their exchequer.

They appeared in any sort of a makeshift theatre, sometimes a barn, horses permitting or frequently the courtyard of an Inn. But the Kembles were nevertheless an illustrious family, they lived greatly and in time through hard work, courage and genius, they lifted themselves to a position of respect and in the case of Sarah Kemble, later Mrs. Siddons, finally to one of reverence.

Sarah was the oldest child. She was born at an Inn that went by the picturesque name of "The Shoulder of Mutton," picturesque that is to a group of strollers to whom a bounteous meal was a rare adventure. The Inn was a gathering place for Welsh farmers and I wonder if possibly her father's company was not acting a play in the courtyard at the very moment when she made her entrance into life. Did the entire company feast that evening on savory mutton by way of celebration or did they go hungry in order that the midwife or doctor might be paid? I like to think, however, that the family was in funds so that Roger could set up beer for all the farmers who years later were perhaps to be numbered among her audience.

Roger Kemble was a Roman Catholic, his wife a Protestant. They solved their religious difficulties very amiably by agreeing that all the boys with whom they might be blessed were to be brought up as Catholics. The girls,

Protestants. There were twelve children of which eight survived to go on the stage. But only two attained to star proportions. They were of course, Sarah and John Philip Kemble who was two years her junior. For awhile in the theatrical world, he eventually became monarch of all he surveyed. But before that end was attained there were many hardships and privations to be endured. The family knew hunger even before they knew how to talk.

Sarah was well-educated. She attended school whenever it was possible. But most of her knowledge was derived from her mother. Carefully, patiently, the little mind was molded. Great indeed was that mother who though a wanderer, seldom having a home, was able to gather her little family about her and instill in them a love of home, honor and puritan ideals.

Sarah liked to read, especially Milton. She studied long passages until she could repeat them by heart. Blind Milton it was who taught her to see the beauty of poetry.

In 1773, Sarah Kemble married Henry Siddons, a good-looking young actor who had secured a position in her father's company because of his versatility. He could play either Harlequin or Hamlet with equal facility but, perhaps more important still, he was able to play the part of husband to Sarah in a diminuendo key. In the subsequent career of his wife, little is heard of him, though for awhile after the wedding they both continued under her father's management. During the following years, the Siddons had two children and as far as obtainable records show, their marriage proved a happy one,

[229]

though never was Henry, as an actor, to be compared to the magnificence of his wife.

Mrs. Siddons' first outstanding success was in *Venice Preserved* written by Thomas Otway in 1682. This performance was attended by persons of quality who recognized the quality of her acting. One especially, the Honorable Miss Boyle, afterwards Lady O'Neil, took Sarah under her wing. She welcomed her to her home. Permitted her to wear her costly costumes. Introduced her to people of prominence. So much fuss was made over her that echoes of her perfection drifted to Garrick's ears.

But now, I step aside, so that Mrs. Siddons, herself, may take up the narrative. The quotations are from her own private journals. Thus does she write: "Mr. King, by order of Mr. Garrick, who had heard some account of me from the Aylesbury family, came to Cheltenham to see me in the *Fair Penitent*. I knew neither Mr. King nor his purpose; but I shortly afterward received an invitation from Garrick himself, upon very low terms. Happy to be placed where I presumptuously augured that I should do all that I have since achieved, if I could but once gain the opportunity. I was at that time good-looking; and certainly, all things considered, an actress well-worth my poor five pounds per week. His praises were most liberally bestowed upon me; but his attentions great and unremitting as they were, ended in less than nothing. How was all this admiration to be accounted for consistently with his subsequent conduct? Why thus, I believe; he was retiring from the manage-

ment of Drury Lane, and, I suppose, at that time wished
to wash his hands of its concerns and details. I moreover
had served what I believe was his chief object in the
exaltation of poor me,—and that was, the mortification
and irritation of Mrs. Yates and Miss Younge, whose consequence and troublesome airs were, it must be confessed,
enough to try his patience. As he had now almost withdrawn from it, the interests of the theatre grew, I suppose, rather indifferent to him. However that may have
been, he always objected to my appearance in any very
prominent character, telling me that the fore-named
ladies would poison me, if I did. I of course thought
him not only an oracle, but my friend; and, in consequence of his advice, Portia, in *The Merchant of Venice,*
was fixed upon for my debut; a character in which it
was not likely that I should excite any great sensation.
I was, therefore, merely tolerated. The fulsome adulation
that courted Garrick in the theatre cannot be imagined;
and whoever was the luckless wight who should be hon-
oured by his distinguished and envied smiles, of course
became an object of spite and malevolence. Little did I
imagine that I myself was now that wretched victim.
He would sometimes hand me from my own seat in the
Green Room to place me next to his own. He also se-
lected me to personate Venus, at the revival of the *Jubi-
lee.* This gained me the malicious appellation of Garrick's Venus; and the ladies who so kindly bestowed it
on me rushed before me in the last scene, so that if Mr.
Garrick had not brought us forward with him with his

own hands, my little Cupid and myself, whose appointed situations were in the very front of the stage, might as well have been in the island of Paphos at that moment. Mr. Garrick would also flatter me by sending me into one of the boxes, when he acted any of his great characters. In short, his attentions were enough to turn an older and wiser head. He promised Mr. Siddons to procure me a good engagement with the new managers, and desired him to give himself no trouble about the matter, but to put my cause entirely into his hands. He let me down, however, after all these protestations, in the most humiliating manner; and, instead of doing me common justice with those gentlemen, rather depreciated my talents. This Mr. Sheridan afterwards told me; and said that, when Mrs. Abington heard of my impending dismissal, she told them they were acting like fools. When the London season was over, I made an engagement at Birmingham, for the ensuing summer, little doubting of my return to Drury Lane for the next winter; but whilst I was fulfilling my engagement at Birmingham, to my utter dismay and astonishment, I received an official letter from the prompter of Drury Lane, acquainting me that my services were no longer required. It was a stunning and cruel blow, overwhelming all my ambitious hopes, and involving peril, even to the subsistence of my helpless babes. It was very near destroying me. My blighted prospects indeed induced a state of mind that preyed upon my health, and for a year and a half I was supposed to be hasting to a decline. For the sake of my poor children, however, I roused myself to shake off this despondency, and my endeavors were blest with success, in spite of the degradation I had suffered in being banished from Drury Lane, as a worthless candidate for fame and fortune."

Even though at this time, Sarah Siddons did not please London audiences, in the provinces she was greatly beloved, especially in Bath where some time later she appeared for four successive seasons.

Sarah liked to associate with the nobility, or with people whose wealth permitted them to move in charmed circles. In Bath, she was welcomed everywhere. And she took all the applause seriously. If Sarah had any defect, it was the absence of a sense of humor. She did not know that she was popular because she was a superb actress. Her articulation was very clear and exact. She was an accomplished singer. Often she sang in her plays when the parts permitted. And because she was the toast of the town she was invited everywhere to tea, which was not inappropriate.

Then came an unforgettable year—1782—and London again. The date October tenth. The place Drury Lane. Unfortunately Garrick was gone, which somewhat lessened her jubilance. Sheridan had bought the patent rights to the theatre. She was well advertised and puffed. Her ability was trumpeted about London. The part chosen for her was that of Isabella. But let Sarah tell it in her own words. Could an author have a fairer collaborator?

"I was truly grieved to leave my kind friends at Bath, and was also fearful that the power of my voice was not equal to filling a London theatre. My friends, too, were doubtful; but I soon had reason to think that the bad construction of the Bath Theatre, and not the weakness of my voice, was the cause of our mutual fears. On the tenth of October, 1782, I made my first new appearance at Drury Lane, with my own dear beautiful boy, then but eight years old, in Southerne's tragedy of *Isabella*. This character was judiciously recommended to me by my kind friend, Mr. Sheridan, the father of Richard Brinsley Sheridan, who had seen me in that play at Bath. The interest he took in my success was like that of a father."

And it *was* a success, a triumph, absolute and complete. She captured her audience, played upon the emotions, a symphony of which she was the master. Never had the audience beheld such purity of acting.

Of her arrival home that night, she writes: "I reached my own fireside on retiring from the scene of reiterated shouts and plaudits. I was half dead; and my joy and thankfulness were of too solemn and overpowering a nature to admit of words or even tears. My father, my husband and myself sat down to a frugal meat supper in silence uninterrupted except by exclamations of gladness from Mr. Siddons."

The season that followed was one of pronounced success. All London was at her feet. At last she had drunk life to the full and found that it was sweet. No actress of her time, in the opinion of those who saw her, was fit to compare with her. And this opinion has been consistently held even up to comparatively recent years. Brander Mathews has declared that she was "probably the greatest actress the world has ever seen."

At this point, I wish to relate an incident in regard to the beautiful rhinestone necklace which Mrs. Siddons wore when she portrayed the part of *Isabella*. It became, as time went on, a sort of heirloom in the Siddons family. Forty years ago it was the property of Mrs. Scott Siddons, a descendant of Sarah Siddons. Mrs. Scott Siddons was a Shakespearean actress, very beautiful in face and in figure. However, she was much more accomplished as a reader than as an actress. She came to me one day at the old Lyceum Theatre, showed me the necklace which she had inherited, and asked me if I would loan her some money upon it. She would leave the necklace as security. I readily assented, paid her the money and put the necklace in my safe. It was never redeemed. I forgot all about it until I discovered it in my safe about four years ago when Miss Sybil Thorndike, the English actress whom I had known and admired for many years, was playing in this country. I went to her one evening and put the necklace around her neck. I said to her, "Miss Thorndike, I want you to wear this necklace, and when you retire from the stage I hope you will give it to the outstanding English actress who succeeds you, with the request that she bequeath it to the artist who succeeds her, and so on. In this way the necklace may continue down the list of outstanding actresses, carrying with it something of the glory of Sarah Siddons."

19

EDMUND KEAN

1

NO ONE knows exactly when Edmund Kean was born but when he died the whole world mourned. He was born either in 1787 or 1789. Kean, himself, was fond of mystification and at various times he gave various dates as those of his birth. It was ever his custom to change his birthdays to suit his needs. His mother was either Charlotte Tidswell, a member of the old Drury Lane company whom in later years he called aunt, or Nance Carey, a wayward, headstrong actress who usually was a member of strolling companies, playing at provincial theatres or at fairs. Now and then she added to her fortunes by selling flowers, ribbons and knick-knacks which she peddled from door to door.

It is generally accepted as a fact that Nance was really his mother, that she abandoned him when he was a few months old and that thereafter he was brought up by Charlotte Tidswell until maternal instincts once more commenced to stir in Nance's breast for there can be no doubt that he travelled for some time with Nance as soon as he was old and strong enough to stand the hardships of such a life. He was a very beautiful child and helped promote the sale of her flowers. It is said that when he was two years old he appeared in some unknown opera, playing the part of Cupid, at which time one old lady inquired if he were really a living child. He looked as though he were made of wax.

However, his first authenticated appearance on any stage, for there is in existence an old play-bill to prove it, was as Robin in *The Merry Wives of Windsor* at the Theatre Royal, Drury Lane, London, June 8th 1796.

Further credence to the fact that Nance Carey was his mother is given by the fact that in later years, after Kean had become a successful actor, he settled £50 per year upon her. Some historians claim that she hounded him until he did so; that the sole reason for this annuity was an effort on Kean's part to get a bit of peace.

Edmund Kean's father was either Aaron, Moses or Edmund Kean or possibly the Duke of Norfolk. If any belief can be held in the Duke's paternity, then it would explain Miss Tidswell's interest in the child for she was closely associated with the Duke, and many of the songs of the troubadours might have been applied to them. If there was no relationship between Edmund Kean and Miss Tidswell it is hard to understand why she looked after him such a large part of the time. Certainly she did not love him. She beat him frequently and once she chained him to the bed for Edmund had a bad habit of trying to run away. Perhaps that explains his whole fierce life, constantly in rebellion, constantly seeking the something more. He was constantly fleeing from life and yet colliding with it.

Thus while there is some uncertainty as to his mother

it is generally conceded that Edmund Kean, the elder, was his father. The fact that their names were the same meant very little for in the theatrical profession names are slipped on or drawn off at will.

Thus there are numerous fantastic stories about Kean's childhood. Little is definitely known. There can be no doubt, however, that he was a brilliant, carefree, reckless lad. He lived mostly on the borderline of starvation. A good meal was a rare event. Despite this, he romped about, laughed and sang merry songs.

When he was very young, in some way or another, he injured his legs seriously and was forced to wear iron braces until he was eleven years old. Yet when he was an actor of prominence there was nothing wrong with his legs so whatever the trouble was, he grew out of it. He was, nevertheless, constantly embarrassed by his smallness of stature.

His schooling was of the sketchiest, probably not more than a few years. Often he claimed he had gone to Eton, but this must be discounted. Drury Lane was his college and he learned his lessons well.

In appearance he was striking, despite his small stature. His hair was dark, his eyes were black, leading many historians to believe that hidden somewhere in his ancestry there may have been a trace of Jewish blood. Others claimed he resembled an Italian. Certain it is that for a while he lived the life of a gypsy, and that too was not surprising for it was a heritage, assuming that his father really was the elder Edmund Kean; for the elder

[239]

Kean was an actor, too, though never a great one. He was also a playwright and a dancer. But he had no great ability. He excelled in nothing but dissipation. This finally led to periods of madness. One night he walked off the roof of a house. His dramatic exit from this stage of life was made when he was only twenty-three. Yet he had accomplished one thing of importance, if his paternity can be accepted, he had given to the world a son who was to write the name of Edmund Kean in the book of stage immortals.

2

His father's death cut deeply into the mind of the impressionable boy. Thereafter he always had the fear of madness hanging over him. It was an obsession.

For several years, starting in 1802, Kean's activities are shrouded in mystery. They were however undoubtedly spent as a strolling player, acting bit parts in the rural districts of England and Scotland.

In 1804 Kean was playing with Samuel Jerold in the Sheerness company. Mr. Jerold's son who was an accomplished author, has left an account of this period. "Mr. Kean," he writes, "joined the Sheerness company on Easter Monday 1804. He was then still in boy's costume. He opened in *George Barnwell* and *Harlequin* in a pantomime. His salary was fifteen shillings per week. He then went under the name of Carey. He continued to play the whole round of tragedy, comedy, opera, farce, interlude and pantomime until the close of the season. His comedy was very successful. In *Watty Cockney* and *Risk,* and in

EDMUND KEAN AS RICHARD III

From a painting by Sir Joshua Reynolds.

SARAH SIDDONS

the song, *Unfortunate Miss Bailey,* he made a great impression upon the tasteful critics of Sheerness. On leaving the place, he went to Ireland, and from Ireland to Mr. Baker's company at Rochester. It was about this time (as I have heard my father say, who had it from Kean himself), that Mr. Kean, being without money to pay the toll of a ferry, tied his wardrobe in his pocket-handkerchief, and swam the river."

It was in the course of this same visit to Ireland that Edmund Kean first met Mrs. Siddons. He was in Belfast at the time that Mrs. Siddons arrived there to play for a few nights only.

She opened her engagement in a play called *Zara.* Kean played opposite her as *Osmyn.* But instead of studying his part he went with a few friends to a tavern where he spent hours in drinking and carousing with the result that when the curtain rose he gave such an absurd performance, the audience expressed its disapproval. Thereafter he was deeply penitent and when the second play, *Douglas,* was presented he played the part of Young Norval while Mrs. Siddons played Lady Randolph. This time he acted so splendidly that Mrs. Siddons was deeply impressed. Afterward she came to Kean and said, "You have played very well, sir, very well. It's a pity,—but there's too little of you to do anything."

Mrs. Siddons was entirely wrong. There was enough of him to go up among the first rank actors of all time, enough of him to win renown throughout the world. He was large enough to loom up through the ages more than a century after all the giants who trod the boards with him had been forgotten.

The greatness of a man cannot be measured by his stature.

It was once said of Kean in derision, when he was playing the small part of Carney in *Ways and Means:* "He's trying to act: the little fellow's making a part of Carney."

And it was true. Kean made a part of every character he played. Whether it was important or not to the audience, *to him* it was important. That was all that mattered. It was thus that he built up such unforgettable parts as Shylock and Othello.

But I am getting ahead of my story. When I attempted to write an article about Edmund Kean I was afraid he would get out of hand. Kean was always hard to manage He still is, even in biographical notes.

3

In the year 1806 he was once more in London Through the help of Miss Tidswell he secured a contrac to play bit parts at the Haymarket Theatre. One of hi first appearances was in *Hamlet.* But he was as far fror the leading part as the stage would permit.

In *The Mountaineers* he took the part of Keeno, goat-herd. In the afterpiece he was a clown in *Fortune Frolic.*

In 1807, to once more quote Mr. Jerold, "Mr. Kea again appeared at Sheerness; salary one guinea per wee He opened in *Alexander the Great.* An officer in one the stage boxes annoyed him by frequently exclaiming, *Alexander the Little.* At length, making use of his (even then) impressive and peculiar powers, Mr. Kean folded his arms and approached the intruder, who again sneeringly repeated, *Alexander the Little,* and with a vehemence of manner, and a glaring look, that appalled the offender, retorted, 'Yes, with a *GREAT SOUL!*' In the farce of the *Young Hussar,* which followed, one of the actresses fainted in consequence of the powerful acting of Mr. Kean. He continued at that time, and even in such a place, to increase in favor, and was very generally followed, when, at the commencement of 1808, in consequence of some misunderstanding with one of the townspeople, he was compelled to seek the protection of a magistrate from a press-gang employed to take him. Having played four nights, the extent of time guaranteed by the magistrate (Mr. Shrove, of Queensborough), Mr. Kean made his escape with some difficulty on board the Chatham boat, having lain *perdu* in various places until a nocturnal hour of sailing."

From this story it can be seen that Kean had the faculty of arousing people's emotions. He could arouse them to applause or to fury with equal facility. He was one of the most versatile of actors. Though his path was strewn with almost unsurmountable obstacles, he managed to find many moments of enjoyment. There was scarcely a tavern in England where he did not play many return engagements.

In 1808 Kean appeared on the Cheltenham Circuit

and while not the star of the productions he was an important member of the company. How important can be gleaned from the fact that his salary was raised from a guinea to thirty shillings per week. Constant diligence to his work had lifted him to the income of a poorly paid office boy of the present day.

4

In the year 1808 Edmund Kean met Mary Chambers and that meeting was perhaps the most momentous of his life. They met in Gloucester. She was at that time an amateur performer in Beverley's company working without pay. She was assigned the part of Mrs. Mortimer, in a comedy entitled *Laugh When You can.* Edmund Kean was cast in the same play in the character of Sambo, the Black.

When Kean appeared on the stage, Mary Chambers asked, "Who is that shabby little man with such brilliant eyes?"

"Oh, his name is Kean," the manager replied, "a brilliant actor."

However it was not written that Sambo was to prove his ability that night. He did not know his part. He spoke extemporaneously, he floundered in his lines, and displayed an amazing display of verbal gymnastics. Not only did he spoil the part of Sambo but he ruined the part of Mrs. Mortimer as well.

Mary Chambers was furious. "You have ruined my part," she told him. "It is very shameful, sir, that you should come upon the stage and not know a word of your part."

Sambo looked at her in disgust. He made no reply. She wasn't worthy of any. What right had she to criticize him?

Arrogantly he sought out the manager. "Who the devil is she?" he asked.

I don't know what the manager replied but if he had been able to peer a few months into the future, he might have answered, "Why, Mr. Kean, I'm surprised you do not know her, for she is the charming girl who is soon to be your wife."

Three months later, at Stroud, Edmund Kean married Mary Chambers. It was inevitable. Miss Thornton of the Cheltenham Theatre loaned him half a guinea for expenses and the Mistress of *The Dog Tavern* gave them a wedding breakfast free of charge.

Those who knew them both said that he was captivated by her liveliness. The fact that she possessed little ability as an actress was more than compensated by the fact that no woman ever was more competent to play the part of wife and mother. There was a greatness about Mary Chambers that far eclipsed any part that she could attempt in the theatre.

Mary, on her part, forgot Edmund's shabby appearance. She was fascinated by the lustre of his magnificent eyes and by the daily contemplation of his acting genius.

5

For two years beginning June 23rd 1809 he played with the Cherry Company on a circuit that took in Swan sea and Carmarthen in South Wales and Waterford in Ireland.

The first part he assayed with this company was that of Henry in *Speed the Plough*. Next he played the part of Petruchio in *Catherine Petruchio*, a Garrick version of a Shakespearean drama. He won great distinction as Chimpanzee, the monkey, in a pantomime entitled, *Perouse of the Desolate Island* written by John Fawcett and suggested by Kotzebue. Imagine a great artist of whom it could be said that he played either Othello or a monkey with equal facility. Nevertheless, his portrayal of Chimpanzee was an appealing thing and people wept at the little animal's distress. Kean's greatness lay in his wide range of parts. He was a man of a thousand moods. Some parts he played could be shouted aloud, others only whispered. He was the subject of much offstage gossip.

A droll story is told of how on one occasion Kean went home in his monkey's costume and despite the remon strance of Mary, he insisted on sleeping in his make-up varnished face, slightly odorous skins and all. As a human animal he slept, sprawled in the bed while Mrs Kean made up a make-shift bed on a sofa in the nex room.

I can imagine her waking him in the morning, saying, "Mr. Chimpanzee, your porridge is ready."

And perhaps he replied, "Take it away and bring me a cocoanut," or whatever it is that monkeys eat.

Edmund Kean was utterly incorrigible. He gloried in the absurd and the spectacular. Sometimes I wonder if he did not have a good head for publicity.

But though Edmund Kean seemed at times so carefree he was often very gloomy. According to one who knew him, "He used to mope about for hours, walking miles and miles alone, with his hands in his pockets, thinking intensely of his characters. No one could get a word from him. He studied and slaved beyond any actor I ever knew."

Another of Kean's odd roles was that of Friday in *Robinson Crusoe*. He played the part of Faulkland in *The Rivals*. And he was celebrated for his brief sketch entitled *Harlequin* in which he leaped through a balloon of fire.

6

But I am getting ahead of my story. Perhaps there is some excuse for me for it is hard to present an orderly sketch of Edmund Kean so chaotic did he live. He thrived on the new and the unusual. He always wanted a change, something different, new scenes, new faces.

In Birmingham he had been getting on exceptionally well. The theatre was large and well regarded. Mr. and Mrs. Kean had played there for slightly over four months with Watson's Company. The salary of each of them

[247]

was a guinea per week. Thus Mary who was a very indifferent actress was raised to a par with her husband. This to me is one of the most absurd facts in stage history. Along about March 1809 the company moved on to Litchfield where they played eight weeks. In May they returned to Birmingham where Stephen Kemble joined the company. He may not have been a great actor but he was a ponderous one and sometimes when he was supposed to kneel as for instance in *Richard III* when he knelt to Lady Anne he couldn't get up and had to call for assistance, causing Kean to shout with laughter. Kean was never one to worry over hurting people's feelings.

It was about this time that Kean commenced to receive overtures from Cherry. He heeded the appeals for he believed he could better his fortunes by joining Cherry's Company. But Cherry was in Swansea and Kean had no money to get there. He had spent too much money in Red Horse Taverns counting pink elephants. Nevertheless he accepted Cherry's offer although he begged him to send him some money to defray his expenses on the journey. Cherry sent him two pounds. Later he advanced him another two pounds. With this money he paid his lodgings, ten shillings and some other debts. Then accompanied by Mrs. Kean he set out at four o'clock on a fine July morning. They had decided to go afoot toward Bristol. The reason they left so early in the morning was to escape the creditors they had been unable to satisfy.

Mrs. Kean was not at all well so they decided to travel

only about ten or twelve miles per day. Kean carried his theatrical swords over his shoulder and looked with his black hair and dark eyes like a brigand en route for a fortnight's holiday. He was dressed all in blue and a few people they encountered took him for a navy lieutenant which caused him to be respected if nothing else. They had only a single meal the entire day.

At last they arrived at a small village. They had walked the allotted twelve miles. They had a meager supper at a cheap inn and then tumbled into bed, completely exhausted.

So time wore on and at last they arrived at Bristol, utterly penniless. They stopped at a public house called, *The Mulberry Tree*. It was at this time that Kean, in response to a frantic appeal, received his second two pounds from Cherry. I wonder what they did, how they existed, while they waited for Cherry's reply to Edmund's letter. And what would they have done if their appeal for funds had been refused.

I am going to pass over the hardships of that journey. The days seemed endless, the nights of short duration. Eventually they reached Swansea and for the moment their tribulations were over.

On September 13th 1809, Kean's first child, a boy, was born. He was named Howard.

Edmund Kean was very happy. He adored the little one. And now he threw even greater vigor into his acting. More and more his conceptions and originality were the subject of much discussion. Few actors have furnished so much ground for argument.

Kean had the faculty of always spending a little more than he earned. He was constantly in debt. To add to his comparatively meager income while he was with the Cherry company, he often gave private entertainments of songs and recitations at the Assembly House which brought him only a trifling return. Sometimes he taught fencing.

While he was still in Waterford, his second son, Charles Kean, was born.

It was during this period of his life that he suddenly decided that he would like to be an author. It is an ailment that effects most of us at some time or other. And so he wrote an afterpiece, in two acts with several songs. It was presented to the manager, acted once or twice for Kean's benefit. Evidently it pleased Kean immeasurable for thereafter he transmitted the play to Miss Tidswell in London. Miss Tidswell was requested to pay the carrying charges, amounting to several pounds sterling. With great hauteur she refused to do so. What subsequently became of the manuscript is an unsolved riddle.

7

On quitting Cherry's company in Ireland, Kean once more became a wanderer, deciding to be a free lance. His first stop was at Whitehaven, but he was unable to get an engagement anywhere and was forced to part with some of his clothes so that he could eat.

Next he went to Dumfries, one of the towns in which he had played as a boy. No one remembered him. Somewhere during his wanderings he had picked up a dog named Daran, a gay companion who trotted merrily along beside his master.

Dumfries is famous because of the glamor of Robert Burns and also for its slowness in making up its mind. To be sure it did honor Robert Burns but not until he was dead. It is small wonder therefore that it was not interested in Edmund Kean who was too much alive.

Kean arrived in the town penniless but he had courage. He rented a room at a public house and made known the fact that he intended giving an entertainment consisting of his usual songs and recitations. It is doubtful if any theatrical engagement in the whole theatrical world ever met with a colder reception for there was only six pence in the house. It is too bad that history does not record the name of that valiant one, that spendthrift who squandered six pence to gaze on the genius of Edmund Kean.

Afterwards Kean was forced to sell some books and other belongings of his wife. With the two pounds thus received he proceeded to Carlisle. Fortunately Mrs. Kean was not with him on that trip to witness his humiliation. She had remained in Dumfries, waiting to join him when his fortunes should show signs of improving. Nevertheless she became impatient and with her two children, joined him at Carlisle. It was a most inopportune moment for Kean had been running into debt with his landlord. The landlord refused to supply the children with food. Fortunately Edmund who was away from the house when his wife arrived, now returned and was able to appease the hunger of the little ones. After that the landlord softened somewhat. He suggested that Kean hire a room and run a benefit for himself. Kean did so. He wrote out handbills and distributed them about the town. His efforts were not in vain. The people of Carlisle flocked to the recitations in sufficient quantities for Kean to pay up his debts.

After leaving Carlisle, the family fortunes steadily declined.

At Penrith they were so destitute that they were forced to part with Daran, the dog, to which Kean had become greatly attached for there was nothing for him to eat. Day followed day in dreadful monotony, footsore, weary, starving but not hopeless. Nothing could daunt Kean's indomitable will. For always he retained faith in himself.

Nothing went right. They continued on to Richmond and then to York. Each day was a counterpart of the preceding one. Kean was on the very threshold of despair but still he would not give up. Why is the path of greatness always tortuous while the road of mediocrity seems to have asphalt smoothness?

Mrs. Kean was so despondent that night after night she used to kneel by the bedside and pray that she and the children might die peacefully in their sleep, never more to awaken into a world that had grown so bleak and desolate.

Yet there was one ray of light for a certain Mrs. Nokes, wife of a dancing teacher in York, heard of their distress and hurried to them. She had long been a friend of the Keans. She talked with Mary and heard of their desperate condition. When she was going she pressed a bit of paper into Mrs. Kean's hand. Not till Mrs. Nokes had gone, did Mary examine it. It was a five pound note.

Nor did Mrs. Nokes' kindness stop there. She proceeded to interest her husband in the Keans. Thereupon he lent Kean the room in which he was accustomed to rehearse his pupils. In this manner Kean was able to clear nine pounds by his readings and songs.

Soon after this, the Keans proceeded to London. It was a long weary journey. But in London, to make up for countless hardships, they were able to visit the theatre where they saw John Philip Kemble and Mrs. Siddons as Cardinal Wolsey and Queen Katherine.

When they returned to their rooms that night, Edmund commenced imitating John Kemble and so realistically that Mary was charmed.

"In all of England," he said, "Kemble is the only man to whom I would play second."

And Mary replied, "You should always be first."

Then Kean grew serious. "I wonder shall I ever walk those boards," he mused. "Will I ever gain as great acclaim as he?"

"Of course you will," Mary declared.

"I must," he cried. "I will. Nothing shall stop me."

And nothing ever did. No obstacle was too great for

him to surmount. But as to finding happiness, that is another story. Edmund Kean always saw the humor in everything. Perhaps, because he was so gifted, he never realized that his life was a tragic success.

Kean next joined the Jack Hughes company at Exeter. Now at last he was playing first-rate parts; Richard, Shylock and Othello. The critics cheered him but it was only when he played Harlequin that he was able to fill the theatre. The part had always been a favorite in the country towns. The people liked his odd costume, his wand and the way he capered about. But the strange part of it all was that Harlequin was always played in pantomime. It stirred the imagination of simple folk. It raised their spirits. It lifted them up until their heads were in the clouds. And as they walked home full of this new wonder which Kean's magic had given them, Kean usually went to *The Red Lion* where he joined a band of gay companions and drank and drank until the cold gray dawn. There was little magic in Kean's step as he returned to his rooms, weary, hoarse from singing ribald songs and disgruntled with everything.

It is recorded that at this time in Exeter, Kean had rooms upstairs over the shop of two spinster sisters named Hake. They were very religious and narrow-minded and they would not have permitted Edmund Kean in their house had they known that he was so frequently in his cups. They lived precisely, without sin, and it would have amazed them had they known that Edmund found most of the sins of this earth very pleasant. I might add that the store downstairs was a china shop and Edmund was like the proverbial bull in it. At the time Kean rented the rooms he was passing through a sober interval but he soon got over that.

One night after Kean had been drinking with great efficiency, a chap with more valor than brains disputed the propriety of his acting. Harlequin was enraged. A battle of words ensued but that was not sufficient for Kean. He wished something more deadly. He challenged his heckler to a duel. Whether his challenge was accepted or not is not definitely known, but presumably it was for Kean still dressed as Harlequin went back to his rooms to get the swords which he usually used when acting Richard. On his way home his anger abated somewhat. Instead of carving his enemy he decided to cut up some capers. In the hall of the house he let out some unearthly cries and started prancing around, laughing heartily. The Misses Hake came out and gazed at this monstrous little figure as though he were some good-natured ghost who had found his way into their sacred halls. At that moment Harlequin made a terrific leap and sailed over the heads of the two frightened ladies at a single bound. Thereupon Mrs. Kean appeared upon the scene and managed to push him into his own room. But she could not constrain him for long for presently he was marching back to *The Red Lion,* swords and all. But no casualties were reported even though Kean remained at the wars for three days.

In 1812 Edmund Kean was in Guernsey. It was here

that he made an amazing discovery. He had preceded Mrs. Kean and the children, acting still with the Hughes company. When Mrs. Kean joined him on the island, he met her at the boat.

"Mary," he cried, "what do you think? I can get brandy here for eighteen-pence a bottle! I can drink it instead of beer!"

His stay in Guernsey was very successful. He played many parts and when he could spare the time he taught dancing. He also held classes for the study of Shakespeare. Historians tell us that at this time he was working so hard, he leaned on brandy for support. Sometimes he leaned too hard and the support gave way, making of him a ludicrous spectacle. In fact he drank so much that the good people of Guernsey became disgusted. They well appreciated his talents but because of his excesses they stayed away from the theatre. Kean was very angry over this. He did not consider himself in any way to blame. He reasoned it was all the manager's fault. When he was supposed to play *Charles I* he refused to show up. Instead he sent Hughes a message to the effect that Charles had been beheaded on his way to the play. Thereupon Hughes gave orders that Kean was not to be admitted again to the theatre. A great many tickets had been sold so Hughes decided to play the part himself. Before doing so he would make a curtain speech explaining that Kean was ill and his doctors would not permit him to appear at the theatre.

Kean heard of this and decided that he would go to

NIBLO'S GARDENS 1845

OLD BOWERY THEATRE

the play to see how Mr. Hughes would acquit himself as an actor. For once the actor would turn critic. On opening night he sat in one of the boxes and as the play was in progress, he suddenly started to applaud and shouted, "Bravo, Hughes." At the sound of that voice I daresay all Hughes' bravado fled from him. From that moment onward it was more like *Charles the Last* than *Charles I*. Hughes forgot most of his lines. The other actors were so angry they jumbled theirs and the audience was so angry that they didn't hear the play anyway, so it did not matter. But the night was not entirely a failure for Kean enjoyed every moment of the evening. To him, *Charles I, Without Edmund Kean* was a great success.

Even after this Mr. Hughes did not dispense with Kean's services for he well knew how great was Kean's ability as an actor. He did however fine him a fortnight's salary. At this Kean registered a loud protest. He had been robbed, he had been victimized. He refused to accompany the company any further. When the others sailed for Weymouth, Kean remained behind. Some wit of the period declared that the presentation of *Charles I* had been ill-advised. Not only did Charles lose his head but the Hughes company had lost its head as well.

Edmund and Mary, with the children, took ship for Devonshire on a dirty little vessel laden with ill-smelling skins. They left the vessel at the small town of Brixham. Once more he hired a room and announced recitations but this time not a single person came. The receipts were not even a sixpence.

Very low spirited, they proceeded on to Exeter and prevailed upon their former landladies, the Misses Hake, to take them in once more. It is a noteworthy proof of Kean's oratory that he was able to beat down all their flocks of objections.

In March 1813 he was once more playing Shylock with some measure of success.

During Kean's second residence at Exeter, he received an offer from a manager named Fisher to play four nights at Teignmouth. Kean accepted. While he was playing the part of *Harlequin* at Fisher's Theatre a certain Dr. Drury sat in the audience. Drury was on his way to London to dine with General St. Leger and Mr. Pascoe Grenfell who was one of the committee managing the famous Drury Lane Theatre.

Dr. Drury was very enthusiastic about Kean's acting. He talked with him when the play was over. He declared that he would use his influence to get Kean an opportunity in London.

Not long after this, Kean received a letter from Dr Drury in which he stated that he had told Pascoe Grenfell of his talents, who thereupon had recommended him to a certain Mr. Whitbread, a London manager. Mr Whitbread had at once written Drury advising him to have Kean proceed at once to London. Kean was overjoyed but unfortunately he had no money to make the trip. To add to his difficulties his son Howard was taken violently ill with whooping-cough aggravated by other complications. In order to make a little money the family went to Barnstaple where Kean was treated kindly by the manager. He was engaged at a salary of two pounds per week. He only stayed a short while for the plays were poorly attended. In despair, he decided to proceed to Dorchester.

Although he had scarcely any money he hired a *post-chaise* in order that he might start his trip like a gentleman. After they had proceeded about a quarter of the way, Kean checked up his finances and decided he would have to dispense with the costly equipage. From that point on Mrs. Kean and Howard, who was growing worse hourly, proceeded by coach while Edmund decided to walk the rest of the way, carrying Charles on his back. It was not the first time he had travelled afoot but it was the first time he had attempted a long journey with a child on his back. At night they stopped at a small roadside inn, where Kean saw that little Charles was fed. Whether or not he had sufficient to buy food for himself is unrecorded. But I daresay he was able to scrape together sufficient money for a glass of strong ale.

The next morning he encountered a company of strolling players, equally as impoverished as himself, who were living up to their name. They were strolling to Dorchester, the only type of transportation they could afford. They were a ragged motley crew but kindly. Though their pocketbooks were lean they had stout hearts. Occasionally they relieved Kean of his burden.

[259]

For miles they took turns carrying the child. At noon of the second day they reached their journey's end, hot, footsore and tired. Mrs. Kean was a trifle provoked because little Charles' clothes were soiled.

"Be thankful we got here at all," said Edmund.

Much to Kean's disappointment the theatre at Dorchester was even more shabby than that at Barnstaple. There were scarcely any tickets sold. To add to his woes, Howard became delirious and seldom had a conscious moment. Poor Kean had no time for weeping. He must act, so that he could take care of his family. But he was almost distraught, for he loved Howard dearly.

He used to dress for his parts at home and wear a long cloak over his costume while he walked to the theatre. On a certain night he acted Octavian in *The Mountaineers*. Mrs. Kean did not accompany him to the theatre but stayed at home to nurse the sick child. Hours passed. Then suddenly Kean appeared, breathless, excited. He could scarcely speak because of his agitation. But at last he managed to cry, "My fortune is made! My fortune is made!"

Then he turned toward the bed on which frail little Howard lay. "If only our boy lives," he said softly, "we shall all be happy."

Later when Mrs. Kean questioned him about what had happened, he told her that that night a stranger had sat in one of the boxes. He did not applaud but seemed very much interested as the play progressed. Later he introduced himself. He was Mr. Arnold, Manager of the Drury Lane Theatre.

The next morning Kean met Mr. Arnold at his hotel. They had breakfast together. Mr. Arnold asked Edmund a few questions about his experiences but they had not been together long before he gave him a contract to act at Drury Lane. The contract was for three years. The first year his salary was to be eight pounds per week. The second year nine and the third ten.

"I am sorry," Mr. Arnold mused, "that you are not half a head taller. With your fine Italian face, if you were, your fortune would be made."

Kean was elated. In all his life he had never been happier. He rushed home to tell his wife the joyful news. The thing they had dreamed of for so long was about to come true. Their cup of happiness was filled to the brim.

Two days later, little Howard died.

On November 25th 1813, he wrote the following letter to Dr. Drury, his benefactor: "The joy I felt three days since at my flattering prospects of future prosperity is now obliterated by the unexpected loss of my child. Howard, sir, died on Monday morning last. You may conceive my feelings, and pardon the brevity of my letter. Mr. Arnold saw me play Alexander and Octavian. This heart-rending event must delay me longer in Dorchester than I intended. Immediately I reach London, I will again, and I hope with more fortitude, address you. In the midst of my affliction I remember your kindness, and, with the greatest respect, sign myself yours, etc., Edmund Kean."

8

Kean arrived in London in early November 1813 in his usual condition—penniless. He felt blue, despondent. His wife was still in Dorchester with Charles. He was forced to borrow eight pounds from the treasurer of Drury Lane in order that they might join him. They did so as soon as they received the transportation money.

Kean was deeply grieved by the coldness with which he was received in London. None of the other members of the company went out of their way to be kind to him. One actress so huge that she seemed as though she were preparing to play the part of a pachyderm, attempted to ridicule him in the same manner as Mrs. Siddons. Beholding him at morning rehearsals in which he was assigned no part, she said, "The little man in the great capes is here again. Poor little fellow! He'll be smothered in his capes. He wants to come out! What is the stage coming to? Who will come next?"

One of the greatest of his biographers makes the following comment on this incident: "We forget who came next; but we remember, that (with a single exception) no one has ever come near him."

Time wore on. Edmund Kean was still neglected. He couldn't understand why he was so completely ignored. He made several attempts to see the manager. But he was always too busy to talk to him. Edmund persisted and finally one morning Mr. Arnold deigned to see him. He was in a very bad humor. A certain Mr. Elliston of Barnstaple claimed that Kean could not act for Arnold because of a previous contract with him. There was nothing to this contention. Kean tried to explain the matter to Arnold who refused to believe the story. In despair Kean wrote to Elliston begging him to tell the truth in the matter. He tried to make his letter as agreeable as possible but as he wrote he lost his temper and declared that he would rather starve to death than return to Barnstaple. To this extraordinary epistle there was no reply, which is not surprising. In the meantime he received no money from Drury Lane except the eight pounds he had borrowed.

For two months Kean remained at his lodgings, 21 Cecil Street, Strand, with no income whatsoever. With him was his wife and Charles. They were reduced to the utmost poverty. They pawned their clothes to eat. Not infrequently they were supplied with food by the Williams sisters with whom they lodged. It was nevertheless a systematic course in starvation. They made an effort to have meat at least once a week but they were not always successful. They ate the coarsest of foods. They were still too proud to let the true state of their finances be known to the other stage folk that they knew. It would be an acknowledgment of defeat. And defeat was a word that Kean never knew. He had come to London in quest of renown.

Then the unexpected happened. On Wednesday the 26th of January 1814, a day that looms large in theatrical annals, the Drury Lane play-bills announced that "their Majesties' servants" would that evening perform *The Merchant of Venice*. The parts announced were as follows: Portia, Miss Smith; Antonio, Mr. Powell; Bassanio, Mr. Rae; Lorenzo, Mr. Phillips; Lancelot, Mr. Oxberry; Gratiano, Mr. Wrench; and "Shylock, Mr. Kean, from the Theatre Royal, Exeter."

That night was one of the coldest and dreariest of the year. The snow was several feet deep. Most of the good folks of London were in their own homes huddled before their fires. And as for Kean, he was melancholy, sad, a trifle bewildered. His appearance was unheralded. There had been no publicity. No one had sung his praises. He was merely a sallow-faced, friendless little man who for two months had been starved to make ready for his part. He had never rehearsed with the other actors until the morning of the day on which the play was to open.

On that day he was directed to walk through his part. It was ever one of Edmund Kean's virtues that the moment he stepped upon a stage, he became a changed man. His own character slipped from him and he became in truth the very person he was enacting. Happy or sad, cold or dismal, it made no difference. His genius was a flame that carried him through, but through in his own manner. He did not read his parts as any other had done before him. He gave to each an individuality. He clothed them with his own magnificent interpretations.

Mr. Raymond, the stage-manager was there. The other

actors grouped about coldly. There was no friendly smile
on any face. "He will be sure to fail," was the consensus
of opinion.

Kean commenced going through the various speeches
of Shylock, giving his customary inflections and man-
nerisms.

Mr. Raymond was irritated. "This will never do," he
grumbled. "It is an innovation, sir. It is totally different
from anything that has been done on these boards."

"Sir," replied Kean emphatically, "I *wish* it to be so."

"It will not do, Mr. Kean," persisted the manager. "Be
assured of it."

"Well," mused Kean, "I may be wrong. If so the *public* will set me right."

Raymond turned to the other actors and winked. The
wink said as plainly as words, "Let the little man make a
fool of himself."

Kean was very dejected when he went home. The
interlude at the theatre had been anything but satisfactory. But when he reached home his spirits were revived
for Mary had fried him a thick juicy steak and had procured for him a pot of porter. I rather suspect that the
Williams sisters had something to do with the feast, but
what matter? The main thing is that on that auspicious
night, he dined!

After dinner was over, Kean got together his few properties, his wig and collar and costume, and set off through
the snowdrifts to the theatre. Drury Lane that night was
almost deserted. Nevertheless in the audience there were

one or two critics of renown, including Kean's perennial benefactor, Dr. Drury. As Kean walked out on the stage it was apparent that history was to be made that night.

"I could scarcely draw my breath," said Dr. Drury to Kean afterwards, "when you first came upon the stage. But directly you took your position and leaned upon your cane, I saw that all was right."

That night the applause was friendly. He took numerous bows. Probably no man was ever more fitted to play Shylock, with his expressive face, his flashing dark eyes, and just the proper note of asceticism. What a revengeful, sinister Shylock he was!

"Three thousand ducats? Well!" Merely a few words and the audience knew there could be no failure.

As the play continued, the audience fell completely under his spell. He swayed them with a wave of his hand, the inflection of a word. No longer were they in the theatre. They had become part of something vital, real. "Hath not a Jew eyes?" He spat out the words with an awful frenzy, a subdued frenzy, the pent-up wrath against years of indignities.

When the play was over the audience cheered wildly.

Mr. Pope said to him, "You have made a hit tonight, sir."

Mr. Powell said, "You have done wonders, sir. You have saved the theatre."

Mr. Arnold, the manager, was emphatic in his praise. "You have exceeded our expectations, sir," said he. "This play will be repeated next Wednesday."

Edmund Kean trudged back to Mary through the snow. He was hungry no more. There was only one thing to mar the pleasure of victory.

"Oh! that Howard were alive now," he murmured.

Edmund Kean was without a doubt the best Shylock that ever trod the boards. He liked the part because the long loose Oriental dress he wore, made his small, scrawny figure less conspicuous.

On the first night Kean played Shylock at Drury Lane, there was £164 in the box office. On the second night £325 was taken in. After that the 3000 ducats that Shylock talked about was a mere pittance. After Kean played Shylock for the third time the contract which he had agreed to with Mr. Arnold was torn up and a new one handed to him that called for twenty pounds per week, which was a very nice gesture on the part of the management of Drury Lane.

After Edmund Kean had played Shylock for six times, it was decided to present him in *Richard III* to show his versatility. Kean viewed this new part with dismay. He had not minded playing in the provinces, but this was London. How would he make out without the long flowing Oriental costume of Shylock. Now the audience would be more aware of his small size. He dreaded losing the audience he had fought so hard to gain. Nevertheless his performance of Richard, we are told, was "vigorous, brilliant and original." On the 24th of February 1814 more than six hundred pounds were taken in for a single performance.

Edmund Kean received many presents in appreciation of his splendid acting. It was a custom of the times. One anonymous donor sent him a note for a hundred pounds. The Duchess of St. Albans visited him and gave him fifty pounds. There were numerous other grants and then as a climax, some time later, the management of Drury Lane gave him a purse containing five hundred pounds, besides which four of the shareholders gave him a share each in the theatre.

When Kean opened in *Hamlet* on the 12th of March there were six hundred and sixty pounds in the house. More tickets could have been sold had there been more room. Kean's Hamlet, however, was never as brilliant as his Othello or Shylock.

During the run of *Hamlet,* Mrs. David Garrick attended the theatre every night. Later she wrote a letter to Kean requesting him to call upon her. After greeting him, she placed him in her husband's chair. "Henceforth," she said, "that chair will be kept solely for you."

9

During the following years, Kean drank deeply of success. He drank everything else as well. He had become the foremost Shakespearean actor in England but he was still as irresponsible as ever. One man has told of meeting him wandering about the streets, dressed as Richard III. Another relates how he used to ride his horse, the name of which was Shylock, through the London streets at break-neck speed after midnight. Often he rode Shylock up and down the steps of the Drury Lane Theatre. Had the doors been unlocked, he undoubtedly would have ridden right in and galloped up and down the aisles.

I set out to write a few impressions of Edmund Kean and now it is beginning to take on the aspects of a biography, so therefore I will not dwell on his purchase of a yacht or his other extravagances and absurdities. These have all been set down by more capable writers than I.

In the fall of 1820, Edmund Kean visited the United States. His tour was a march of triumph. He reaped a fortune for himself and another for his managers. In New York, several days before he opened, tickets were sold at public auction and they brought fabulous amounts.

His first American appearance was in *Richard III* during November 1820. Then he went on a tour of all the northern states that lasted until August 1821.

On his return to London he was met by the entire Drury Lane Company at Barnet, in the suburbs. Kean greeted them with serious mien.

"Before you say a word, my merry men," he cried, "behold! Fall down and kiss this relic. This is the toe-bone of the greatest creature that ever trod this earth— George Frederick Cooke. He was lying in America without a monument until I caused one to be erected over him. Come, down with you all, and kiss this bone!"

One by one the company came forward to fall upon their knees and kiss the ridiculous relic.

[269]

10

To me the most amazing thing in Edmund Kean's life was his jealousy of Charles, his only son. To his dismay on a certain occasion he discovered that Charles had an aptitude for the stage. Mary Kean was proud of the boy's ability. She wanted him to carry on the Kean tradition. But not so Edmund. He flew into a violent rage. He cursed and swore and strode around the house like a madman.

"Sooner than have him be an actor," he cried, "I would cut his throat! I am the only Kean in this family who shall be a great tragedian."

He ordered Charles to give up his theatrical ambitions. Charles stubbornly refused. In fairness to Edmund Kean it must be stated that he was not in the best of health at this time. He had lived violently for years, giving in to countless excesses. The pleasant sins of this world had affected his mind. This was not the same Edmund Kean who had suffered so acutely when Howard, his oldest son, had died. It was a Kean whose finer instincts were blunted. Even his acting had lost something of its perfection. Decay was setting in to spoil the fruits of his genius. Sometimes his memory failed him. He was suspicious of everyone.

During this period he had love affairs with various women. He was always popular with the ladies, due to his magnetic personality and the glamour of the stage that hung about him. One fact in connection with these affairs is very droll. The first love letter was always the same that he wrote to every woman. Thus did he keep free of overtaxing his talents of authorship. He was involved in one scandal and oddly enough I am sure he was blameless in the matter. He was a victim rather than a culprit. Nevertheless the resultant law-suit caused him to lose favor with the English people.

When he again appeared on the stage at Drury Lane, the audience set up such a barrage of catcalls and hisses that the play could not go on. At Edinburgh he was hooted from the stage.

Later he once more appeared in London. This time the people were less hostile. He came forward and made the following speech: "If you expect from me vindication of my private conduct, I fear I shall not be able to furnish one to your satisfaction. I stand before you as the representative of Shakespeare's heroes. The errors I have committed have been scanned by a public tribunal. In that investigation feelings of delicacy prevented the disclosure of circumstances which might have changed the complexion of the case. This proceeded from feelings for others, not for myself. It appears that I stand before you, ladies and gentlemen, a professional victim. I apprehend that this is not done by your verdict. If it is done by a hostile press, I shall endeavor to withstand it—if it is your verdict, I shall bow to your decision, remember with gratitude your former favors, and leave you."

Peace with the audience was thus established but Edmund Kean had not made peace with himself. He was moody, melancholy, chronically nervous. His mind was in chaos. He regained the good graces of his public but never again did his acting take on the fire that had swept him to renown. He knew that something was wrong. Something was missing. He was not contented. In despair he decided to visit America again.

His quarrels with his son continued. "The name of Kean shall die with me," he cried. "It shall be buried with me."

No longer could he get along with his wife or his son. He parted from them. Because Charles would not give up acting he cast him out without a penny. To Mrs. Kean he made an allowance of two hundred pounds per year. Charles Kean was sixteen years old when this final break came.

And the years rolled on. Father and son were both actors but they never met. Kean still suffered acutely from the disgrace of his trial. He was an unhappy, broken man. Charles Kean was a fair actor. He played his parts well enough, but everyone compared him to his father to his own detriment. Charles suffered from a chronic bronchial affection that caused a slight impediment in his speech. More and more Edmund Kean sought comfort in drink. His health broke. He went off to the country for a rest cure. He tried to live temperately and for a while he succeeded. Eventually he purchased a controlling interest in the Richmond Theatre. Nevertheless to everyone it was apparent that his health was breaking. He needed complete rest and quiet, yet he had always

FEDERAL STREET THEATRE

BOOTH'S THEATRE

lived violently. Excitement was food for him. He became so weak that he could scarcely play his part. Once after acting the part of Richard III at Covent Garden he was too weak to walk off the stage after the final curtain. He would have fallen if some other members of the company had not come to his assistance and practically carried him to the Green Room.

11

Charles Kean played for about three years in America, returning to England in 1833. It was then that Mr. Laporte, the manager of Covent Garden, conceived of a clever idea. He would present *Othello,* with Edmund Kean portraying the part of Othello and Charles playing Iago. The fact that the two were known to be enemies would act as a spur to public interest. And so it was arranged. I would like to know what argument Laporte gave to win over the approval of Edmund to the enterprise. Perhaps the reason was very simple. Perhaps he was suffering from remorse, reaching out willingly at this opportunity for a reconciliation. I can well imagine that Charles Kean was eager to act with his father. It must have been one of the most romantic nights in all stage history when they opened. Edmund was so weak that he could scarcely stand.

He sat in his dressing room, weak and shivering. "I am very ill," he murmured. "I am afraid I shall not be able to act."

According to his biographer, Mr. Charles Kemble was

there and cheered him up. I wonder if Mary Kean, too, was somewhere in the audience, for even though Mary was living away from him, in spirit she was ever near him. No other man existed so far as she was concerned. She understood Edmund better than anyone, better than he even understood himself.

A certain Mr. Warde stood in the wings dressed as Othello, to take up the part in case Edmund should collapse.

And the curtain rose on the first act. After the first scene was over, Edmund seemed in good spirits.

"Charles is getting on tonight," he commented. "He's acting very well. I suppose it is because he is acting with me."

But Edmund was very tired. Between each scene hot brandy and water was given to him to brace him up.

As the third act approached, he was very feeble.

"Mind, Charles," he directed, "that you keep before me. Don't get behind me in this act. I don't know that I shall be able to kneel; but if I do, lift me up."

Weaker and weaker he became as the play advanced. Then came the celebrated farewell speech which he uttered with all his old-time pathos but at its conclusion his head sank on his son's shoulder.

"Charles, I am dying," he whispered.

The audience sat stunned. Everyone in that house knew they were witnessing tragedy that night that they would never witness again though they lived centuries. They carried him to his dressing room, cold and still.

[274]

scarcely breathing. He knew nothing of what was going on about him. Yet somehow for a brief moment he was at peace, for his son was with him.

A week later he was well enough to be taken back to his home in Richmond. But his acting days were over. Slowly the flame of his life was flickering out. From both ends the candle had burned and there was very little left. Nevertheless he gradually improved in health until he was able to totter feebly about. One day when it was bleak and stormy he made a brief visit to the home of Miss Tidswell. On his way back he caught a chill. He was so cold that he went to bed. But the cold followed him. He drank hot brandy but he could not get warm. In the following days he dozed a great deal, arousing himself at infrequent intervals.

In one of these moments of wakefulness, he wrote a letter to his wife.

"My dear Mary, Let us no longer be fools. Come home. *Forget* and *forgive!* If I have erred, it was my head, not my heart, and most severely have I suffered for it. My future life shall be employed in contributing to your happiness; and you, I trust, will return that feeling, by a total obliteration of the past. Your wild, but really affectionate husband, Edmund Kean."

In response to his letter, Mary came to him at once. For seven years they had lived apart, but they were apart no longer. Charles Kean was also there and through his endeavors the little family's reunion was made complete.

But Edmund's life was fast ebbing from him. He took

[275]

but little food. Hour after hour he lay there gazing into space. What were his thoughts? Did he live over again all the sufferings of his early years? Or did he remember only his triumphs? Who can say?

Occasionally he felt a bit better. In these brief moments he acted again his old parts, with Charles as the only listener. But these intervals became fewer and fewer.

Edmund Kean died quietly in his sleep May 15th 1833.

12

Edmund Kean possessed many faults but he had supreme courage, an indomitable will. He gave vast sums of money to charity and never turned away from anyone in need. It can be truthfully said of him that he gave an impulse to acting, stimulating it at a moment when it was becoming anemic. Kean infused rich red blood into the drama. He portrayed his characters vividly, strikingly. He was an artist who drew his pictures with strong, sure, deft strokes. Like David Garrick, he dignified a stage when he stepped upon it. When he quitted it the whole world mourned.

BIBLIOGRAPHY

BIBLIOGRAPHY

Account of the Life of that Celebrated Tragedian, Mr. Thomas Betterton. London: J. Robinson, 1749

ALGER, WILLIAM ROUNSEVILLE: *Life of Edwin Forrest.* Philadelphia: J. B. Lippincott & Co., 1877

Biographia Dramatica; or, A Companion to the Playhouse. 3 Volumes. By DAVID ERSKINE BAKER to the year 1764; ISAAC REED, F.A.S., to the year 1782; and STEPHEN JONES to the year 1811. London: Longman, Hurst, Rees, Orme and Brown, 1812

BLACK, W.: *Goldsmith.* London: Macmillan & Co., 1878

BOADEN, JAMES: *Memoirs of Mrs. Siddons.* London: H. Colburn, 1827

CAMPBELL, THOMAS: *Life of Mrs. Siddons.* London: E. Wilson, 1834

CIBBER, COLLEY: *An Apology for the Life of Mr. Colley Cibber, Comedian; Written by Himself.* London: J. Watts, 1740

CLARKE, ASIA BOOTH: *Passages, Incidents and Anecdotes in the Life of Junius Brutus Booth By his Daughter,* New York: H. L. Hinton, 1870

CLARKE, MRS. ASIA BOOTH: *The Elder and the Younger Booth.* Boston: J. Osgood & Co., 1882

COLLIER, J. PAYNE: *History of English Dramatic Poetry to the Time of Shakespeare: and Annals of the Stage to the Restoration.* London: John Murray, 1831

COTTON, WILLIAM: *The Story of the Drama in Exeter, 1787-1823, with Reminiscences of Edmund Kean.* London: Hamilton, Adams & Co., 1887

D'AVENANT, SIR WILLIAM: *The Dramatic Works of.* 5 Volumes. Edinburgh: W. Peterson, 1872-1874

D'AVENANT, SIR WILLIAM: *Select Poems of, with a Life of the Author,* By EZEKIEL SANFORD, in *The Works of British Poets.* Philadelphia: 1819-1823

[279]

BIBLIOGRAPHY

D'AVENANT, SIR WILLIAM: *Works of,* Edited by MARY D'AVE-
NANT. London: Henry Herringham, 1673

DAVIES, THOMAS: *Memoirs of the Life of David Garrick.* London: The Author, 1780

DOBSON, AUSTIN: *Collected Poems.* New York: E. P. Dutton &
Co., 1913

DOBSON, AUSTIN: *Life of Oliver Goldsmith.* London: W. Scott,
1888

Frank Leslie's Illustrated Newspaper: New York, Vol. 2—1856

FORSTER, J.: *Life and Times of Oliver Goldsmith.* London:
Ward, Lock & Co., 1862

GAISFORD, JOHN: *The Drama in New Orleans.* New Orleans:
J. B. Steele, 14 Camp Street, 1849

GILDON, CHARLES: *The Life of Mr. Thomas Betterton.* London:
R. Gosling, 1710

GOLDSMITH, OLIVER: *The Bee, a Collection of Essays.* London:
J. Sharpe, 1819

GOLDSMITH, OLIVER: *Essays.* London: Printed for T. Wills By
C. Whittingham and Sold by D. Symonds, 1803

GOLDSMITH, OLIVER: *Gems of Goldsmith: The Traveller, The
Deserted Village, The Hermit, with Notes.* New York: S. R.
Wells & Co., 1880

GOLDSMITH, OLIVER: *Miscellaneous Works,* in 5 Volumes, *with
some account of his Life and Writings.* Baltimore: F. Lucas,
Jr. and J. Cushing, 1816

GOLDSMITH, OLIVER: *She Stoops to Conquer; or The Mistakes
of a Night.* London: F. Newberry, 1773

GOLDSMITH, OLIVER: *The Citizen of the World; or Letters from
a Chinese Philosopher, residing in London to his friends in
the East.* London: Privately printed for the Author and sold
by J. Newberry, 1762

GOLDSMITH, OLIVER: *The Good Natur'd Man: A Comedy as
performed at the Theatre Royal.* Covent-Garden. London:
W. Griffen, 1768

GOULD, THOMAS R.: *The Tragedian.* New York: Hurd and
Houghton, 1868

HARRISON, GABRIEL: *Edwin Forrest, the Actor and the Man.*
Privately Printed. Brooklyn, N. Y., 1889

BIBLIOGRAPHY

HAWKINS, F. W.: *The Life of Edmund Kean*. London: Tinsley Bros., 1869

IRVING, WASHINGTON: *Life of Goldsmith*. New York: Harper & Bros., 1840

KIRKMAN, JAMES THOMAS: *Memoirs of Charles Macklin*. London: Lackington, Allen and Co., 1799

LOCKE, ROBINSON: *Collection of Dramatic Scrap Books*. Toledo: 1920

MACREADY, WILLIAM CHARLES: *Reminiscences and Selections from his Diaries and Letters*. Ed. by Sir Frederick Pollack. New York: Macmillan & Co., 1875

MEDLEY, MAT: *(Anthony Aston) The Fool's Opera*. London, 1731

MOLLOY, JOSEPH FITZGERALD: *The Life and Adventures of Edmund Kean*. London: Downey & Co., 1897

NICHOLSON, WATSON: *Anthony Aston, Stroller and Adventurer*. South Haven, Michigan: The Author, 1920

OLDYS, WILLIAM: *Choice Notes*. Privately Printed with a Memoir by W. J. Thoms. London: 1862

OTWAY, THOMAS: *The Poetical Works of Thomas Otway, with the Life of the Author*. London: C. Cooke, 1797

PEPYS, SAMUEL: *Diary and Correspondence*. 6 Volumes. London: Becker and Son, 1875-1879

PERCY, T.: *The Life of Dr. Goldsmith*. London: J. Swan, 1774

PRIOR, JAMES: *The Letters of Oliver Goldsmith*. Philadelphia: E. L. Carey and A. Hart, 1837

PROCTOR, BRYAN WALLER: *The Life of Edmund Kean*. London: E. Moxon, 1835

Rachel, Memoirs of, By MADAME DE B—. London: Hurst and Blackett, 1858

REES, JAMES: *Life of Edwin Forrest*. Philadelphia: T. B. Peterson & Bros., 1874

SEILHAMER, GEORGE O.: *History of the American Theatre*. Philadelphia: Globe Printing House, 1888

STOPES, CHARLOTTE CARMICHAEL: *Burbage and Shakespeare's Stage*. London: A. Moring Ltd., 1913

STUART, WILLIAM: *Reviews of Plays of Edwin Forrest:* New York *Tribune:* March, 1855

TAINE, H. A.: *History of English Literature,* Trans. from the

BIBLIOGRAPHY

French By H. Van Laun: London: Chatto and Windus, 1897

Theatre Magazine, Edited by DESHLER WELCH. New York: March 1886-June 1890

TUCKERMAN, HENRY THEODORE: *Edmund Kean, the Actor.* Biographical Essays. Boston, 1857

WEGLIN, OSCAR: *The Beginning of the Drama in America. The Literary Collector.* Vol. 9—pp. 177-181. Greenwich, Conn., 1905

INDEX

INDEX

[285]

INDEX

INDEX

[287]

INDEX

INDEX

INDEX

INDEX

INDEX

INDEX

INDEX

INDEX

Weber, Joe, 50
Weber and Fields, 44
Weber and Fields' Music Hall, 49
Wegelin, Oscar, 4
Welch, Deshler, 106
Wessels, Wessel, 7
Westminster Abbey, 87, 183, 192
Wetmore, Prosper M., 27, 28
"When Burbage Played," 173
Whiffen, Mrs. 127
Whitbread, Mr., 258
White, Richard Grant, 49
White, Stanford, 49
"White Horse Tavern, The," 100
White Star Line, 101, 102
Whitney's Gang, 7
Wickeham School, 1
Wilde, Oscar, 2, 167, 168
William the Conqueror, 174
Williams Sisters, 263, 265
Williamsburgh Theatre, 12
Wilson, Alexander, 17
Wilson, Francis, 44, 51
Winter Garden Theatre, 90
Winter, William, 113, 116
"Winter's Tale, A," 99

"Wits, The," 186
Wolsey, Cardinal, 101, 160, 161, 178, 253
Wood, Anthony, 182
Wood, Warren, 21
Wood, William B., 21
Woodhull, 28, 29
Wood's Museum, 49
Wood's Theatre, 21
Wotton, Henry, 178
Wrench, Mr., 264

Yates, Miss, 231
York, Duke of, 194
York Theatre, N. Y., 57
Young, Edward, 77
Young, John Russell, 10
"Young Hussar," 243
Young Norval, 20, 241
"Young Werther," 168
Younge, Miss, 231.

Zanza, 21
Zaphna, 21
Zara, 241
Zoffanij, 209, 210